t

Frank Gille/René Marks

Snowboarding
Make a Perfect Start

Meyer & Meyer Sports

Original title: Snowboard Perfect
Aachen: Meyer und Meyer Verlag, 2000
Translated by James Beaches

British Library Cataloguing in Publication Data
A catalogue for this book is available from the British Library

Frank Gille/René Marks
Snowboarding: Make a Perfect Start
– Oxford: Meyer und Meyer, (UK) ltd., 2002
ISBN 1-84126-058-4

All rights reserved, especially the right to copy and distribute, including the translation rights. No part of this work may be reproduced – including by photocopy, microfilm or any other means – processed, storedelectronically, copied or distributed in any form whatsoever without the written permission of the publisher.

© 2002 by Meyer & Meyer Sport (UK) Ltd.
Aachen, Adelaide, Auckland, Budapest, Graz, Johannesburg,
Miami, Olten (CH), Oxford, Singapore, Toronto
Member of the World
Sports Publishers' Association
www.w-s-p-a.org

Printed and bound in Germany
by Druckpunkt Offset GmbH, Bergheim
ISBN 1-84126-058-4
E-Mail: verlag@meyer-meyer-sports.com
www.meyer-meyer-sports.com

CONTENTS

1 Snowboarding - A Way of Life	7
2 The History of Snowboarding - On the Trail of the Pioneers	13
3 The Right Equipment for Every Snowboarder Type	19
3.1 The Different Types of Boards	19
Freestyle Boards	21
Freeride Boards	22
Freecarving Boards	23
Race Boards	24
3.2 The Board in Detail	25
3.3 Bindings and Boots - A Functional Unit	29
Shell Bindings with Soft Boots	30
Plate Bindings with Hard Boots	31
Step-in Bindings	32
Step-in Boots	33
3.4 Functional 'Clothes Maketh Man'	34
The Outfit	34
Useful Accessories	37
4 Starting Snowboarding - Let's Go!	41
4.1 First Steps with the Board	42
From the Standing Position to Roller-skating	42
4.2 Basic Exercises on the Board	52
From the Basic Position to Diagonal Running	52
4.3 Snowboarding Technique I - The First Downhill Attempt	60
4.4 Snowboarding Technique II - Advanced Manoeuvres	62
4.5 Workshop - Easier Snowboarding	72
Learning Using Variations	72
4.6 Suitable Equipment for Better Snowboarding	77
5 Sports, Action & Fun	81
5.1 Competitive Snowboarding	81
Racing	84
Freestyle	87
Boardercross - Freeriding	90

	5.2	Fun sport - Personal Styles 93
		Freecarving - Racy Turns on the Piste 93
		Freeriding - Cross-country Snowboarding 96
		Freestyle - Tricks and Jumps 104

6 Over the Edge and Beyond 115
	6.1	The Snowboarder's Summer Season 115
		Wakeboarding 115
		Sandboarding 118
	6.2	Snowboarding Camps - Snow & Fun 121
	6.3	Virtual Snowboarding - Internet & Co 124

7 ....and Everything Else that's Important! 131
	7.1	The Ideal Snowboarding Regions 131
	7.2	Snowboarding Courses - Up onto the Board 136
		The Right Type of Snowboarding School 137
		Courses 138
	7.3	Hired Equipment 141
	7.4	Snowboarding for Children - Fun Learning 142
	7.5	Snowboarding - With Safety 150
		Safe Snowboarding 150
		Equipment Safety Checks 153
		The 10 FIS-Rules for Skiers and Snowboarders 155

8 Pure Information 157
	8.1	Snowboarding Glossary 157
	8.2	Internet Addresses 162
		Acknowledgements 163
		Photo & Illustration Credits 164

1 SNOWBOARDING – A WAY OF LIFE

From the beginning to the middle of the 80s, many winter sports followers just gaped as several wild young types, dressed in sloppy clothing with brightly coloured boards, suddenly appeared on "their" ski pistes. This new piece of sports equipment irritated the winter sports' 'establishment', not only because of the outlandish snowboarding outfits, but because of the strange way they moved, which reminded one very much of surfing, but on snow.

Just like many trendy types of sport, the origins of snowboarding also stem from the USA, where, in the 70s, several inspired people spent all summer working so that in winter they could ride on home-constructed boards. A great deal of pioneering spirit went into this, thus promoting snowboarding even further. After its introduction into Europe, and largely due to the 'example' that these pioneers set with their individual efforts, snowboarding has become a fascinating sport - moreover a kind of philosophy - a way of life.

So what is it that actually makes snowboarding so fascinating?
To be able to glide down a fresh, deep, snowy slope on a day with clear skies, hearing the wind whistling in your ears, and to be able to carve out your path as you swing in rhythmic curves - it is this feeling of freedom that every snowboarder experiences. It is the gliding sensation that fascinates numerous leisure seekers coming from other types of sport. Irrespective of whether it is catching the wind and surfing down high waves, or being able to reach speeds of up to 30 mph using one's own efforts on in-line skates, it is the same thing which unifies everyone - being able to move freely and almost weightlessly.

The similarity to skateboarding also makes snowboarding attractive to most. Just like the skateboarder, the "freestyler" can try out numerous new tricks and face the challenge of daring jumps in the half-pipe. Personal creativity and development of one's individual style all play a part in forming the character of the freestyle boarder in his sport, and above all heightens the fun-factor.

The snowboarder can also experience an awful lot on artificial slopes. With the wind rushing past your ears as you speed down through extreme curves and into radical turns, the breathtaking scope of this dynamic sport really comes into its own.

SNOWBOARD

8

Free as a bird (Photo: René Marks)

SNOW BOARD

Whether it is the fast turns, clever jumps or simply the experience of freedom with nature and playing with the elements in this individual sport, snowboarding has something to offer everyone. Because of the versatility of the different snowboard types, active marketing and a slight increase in the number of snowboarding schools available, a number of spectators of the sport, who at first were a bit apprehensive to have a go, have overcome their inhibitions and are actively taking part. Even devoted skiers are giving it a go and climbing onto the 'planks', which mean so much for an increasing number of winter sportsmen and women. Once they have found a taste for the new-found form of movement, many of them are staying with snowboarding and some are even leaving their skis at home forever.

Following the enthusiasm, which the board has drummed up in the meanwhile, and the fact that snowboarding gained Olympic recognition in 1998, this one-time slightly disreputable sport has become socially acceptable. Snowboarding has finally won a place as a winter sport and is no longer a game for kids but something for the whole family. For example, in Germany, the home of the authors, there are now about 300,000 active snowboarders, with about 5 million worldwide, and there appears to be no end to the boom. With the ever-increasing number of snowboarders about, the scene in the Alps has also changed. Activity on the slopes has become more colourful and many of the winter sports resorts have adjusted to the new 'customers' and welcome them with open arms. The really gripping question for the 21st century is: "Who will follow the snowboarders?"

SNOWBOARD

10

SNOWBOARD

11

The pioneers of "Freestyle" - the skateboarders (Photo: René Marks)

◀ *Pure action - a windsurfer in waves (Surfer is Josh Stone / Photo: Jono Knight)*

◀ *Feeling alive – the surfer Shane Brevan (Photo: Mike Newling)*

Gliding on asphalt - In-line Skate Racing (Photo: René Marks) ▶

Sherman Poppen (Rider: Markus Hurme / Photo: Trauma)

2 THE HISTORY OF SNOWBOARDING - ON THE TRAIL OF THE PIONEERS

The scene is a backyard garage somewhere in Michigan/ USA during the winter of 1965. On the workshop bench there are several screwdrivers, a saw and the remains of an old water ski. A man fixes a leash onto a funny looking plastic plank fitted with a fin and, satisfied, places it up against the wall. As he goes out he glances up again at some of the old surfing posters hanging on the walls.

This is how the birth of the snowboard could have been. Only Sherman POPPEN knows exactly just why and under what circumstances this type of board came into being. The surfer's winter hibernation had probably been the reason why he came to carry out this great pioneering act.

It was in the winter of the same year that he began to plummet down the mountains on this plastic board, similar to a pair of water skis, with its rider only attached to it by the leash. This surfing enthusiast applied for a patent a little later, calling the forerunner of the snowboard by the name "SNURFER" - a combination of the words 'snow' and 'surfing'. Thus he laid the corner stone for the development of a new type of winter sport.

In the following year the company Brunswick Sports Goods, as more than ample reward for his pioneering spirit, took up his daring idea and produced thousands of the 1.2 metre plastic board with a middle fin and a leash for the price of 15 dollars.

Sherman POPPEN, the father of the snowboard, and his followers would have had tremendous fun on fresh snow-decked slopes. On today's prepared slopes in the ski resorts, the board with its middle fin would have been rather less suitable. The desire to ride down the ski slopes and pistes was probably the catalyst that heralded the development of the snowboard in the USA 12 years later. Jake CARPENTER, Dimitrije MILOVICH and the once World Champion skateboarder Tom SIMS began the production of more snowboards in 1977. While the two surfers MILOVICH and SIMS experimented with boards similar to those used in surfing, BURTON stumped for a board made of wood similar to the 'snurfer' type. On the top surface he mounted bindings, like those used on water skis, with the rider standing on the board sideways. Encouraged by the good performance of his boards, Jake BURTON founded his own snowboard firm in Londonderry, Vermont and started mass-producing them. A little later Tom SIMS also took up on the same basic idea. The original board has been, without doubt, the basis for all further developments right up to the present day.

BURTON as well as SIMS with their snowboard firms have been very successful in the sphere even up to today.

Despite many run and lift companies in the USA and Europe banning them, the number of snowboarding enthusiasts has continued to increase. In 1981 the first snowboard races took place in North America, in which Tom SIMS very successfully took part. Although it sounds rather exotic, the first national snowboard association - JSBA - was founded in Japan in 1984. At the beginning of the Eighties, the snowboard following was increased by skateboarders changing over, particularly in Europe. A very active snowboarding community quickly developed.

Borrowing from ski technology, and with a good deal of inventiveness on the part of outsiders, steel edges and plate bindings were introduced into snowboarding. Safety was subsequently improved as was the suitability of the board on ski pistes. Together, these factors led to a lifting of some of the ban restrictions, so that there was a continual increase in the number of followers.

In Germany, homeland of the authors, the "Deutsche Snowboard-Dachverband (DSDV)" (Main German Snowboard Organisation) was formed in Munich in 1988 and was the first organisation to represent the interests of all snowboarders in the country.

In 1989 we saw the first German Championships taking place and this proved to be a real highlight. To professionalise the sport in the long run, it was necessary to obtain international agreements.

Between 1990 and 1993 the "International Snowboard Federation (ISF)" was formed and following this there was a worldwide decision to combine all championships into the ISF Pro World Tour. The highlight of all this activity was when the first official ISF World Snowboard Championship was carried out. The great increase of snowboarders and the specific interest of industry now demanded that the established skiing associations should be included in the plan.

In 1994 the ISF decided to stage its own World Cup Series, and crowned its activities in 1996 by holding the first ISF World Championship in Lienz, Austria. In Germany three organisations competed for the favours of the snowboarders. These were the DSDV, the German national subsidiary of the ISF and the FIS (the

Nicola Thost - the first Olympic winner in the Half-pipe (Photo: Nitro)

"Deutscher Ski-Verband (DSV)" (German Skiing Association).

The development of snowboarding was damaged by this multi-lane approach for the bid for the lead and it wasn't until the sport was included in the winter programme for the Olympic Games in Nagano in 1998 that a favourable change came. The heads of the association came to a mutual agreement to form and enter a joint national team. In the Winter Olympic Games of 1998 two German riders led the medallion race. Nicola Thost dominated the field in the Half-pipe and easily won the Gold Medal. In the downhill series Heidi Renoth won the Silver Medal.

This was greeted warmly by the public and the increased media interest around the world helped snowboarding to make the long desired breakthrough. This breakthrough gave the "green light" in all respects for the world of snowboarding.

1965	Sherman POPPEN from Michigan, USA develops his "Snurfer" out of plastic with its leash
1966	Snurfer competitions held in the USA
1977	Jake BURTON CARPENTER builds a board out of wood with a binding; Tom SIMS and Dimitrije MILOVICH on boards similar to the construction of surfing boards
1981	In North America the first snowboard races are held
1982	The first US Snowboarding Championship is held
1983	Snowboards go into production in Europe
1984	First national snowboard association formed in Japan
1988	First national snowboard association formed in Germany (DSVD based in Munich)
1989	First German Snowboarding Championships
1990	ISF formed as the first worldwide snowboarding association
1993	Merger of the European, North American and Japanese Snowboarding Competitions to form the ISF Pro World Tour. First official ISF World Championship held in Ischgl, Austria

SNOWBOARD

1994   IFS, the International Skiing Association, decides on running a World Cup Series
1995   Snowboarding is included in the Winter Olympic Games programme at Kairuzawa, Japan
1996   The first FIS World Championship is held in Lienz, Austria
1998   Snowboarding is added as a discipline in the 1998 Winter Olympic Games in Nagano, Japan
1999   FIS World Championships held in Berchtesgaden, Germany

Well-equipped for snowboarding (Photo: René Marks)

3 THE RIGHT EQUIPMENT FOR EVERY SNOWBOARDER TYPE

Spurred on by the sustained boom for snowboarding in recent years, the snowboarding industry has seen to it that the snowboarder's demands will be met in the next century.

Accordingly there are varying different types of snowboard, each designed for a different kind of use. The construction of the snowboard has been influenced by suggestions from the professionals and by test sessions, comparing new types with the 'normal' board, to optimise them further. Lighter boards, a new form of inner core as well as the optimum shape of the sidecut of the board are all main themes to make the performance characteristics better for next winter's new boards.

The invention of the step-in system has brought about several revolutionary new patents for bindings and footwork in the last two years. The next chapter goes into such vexed questions as to how the snowboard layman finds his way round the various differences in equipment, and whether it is worth buying everything new that comes onto the market.

3.1 The Different Types of Boards

For every newcomer to snowboarding, sooner or later he will ask himself the question, "Which board is actually the right one for me and my demands?" The question is equally applicable to those who are already well into the sport and are looking to buy new equipment.

By the time that the potential buyer gets into the sports shop and is faced with an absolute mountain of equipment, he will note that every board is the right one for him. When choosing the right board the important thing is to know what type of ride one is seeking. In the course of the 'history of snowboarding', many different kinds of style have been developed, among which, in the meanwhile, there are even custom-built boards. Therefore, first of all, one must decide which style of snowboarding one wants to follow, and then look for a suitably matching board.

(Photo: René Marks)

Style and boards are divided into four categories; freestyle, freeride, freecarve and race, whereby the difference between them flows from the one to the other.

When buying a board, besides choosing the right type of board, there are a few other important factors to take into account such as the correct length, breadth and flexibility. On top of this, the rider's weight as well as the effective length of the board's side rails play a decisive role in the selection of a really optimum piece of equipment.

In the following paragraphs there is a systematic overview of corresponding snowboarding styles and the suitable board with its individual characteristics for each style.

Freestyle Boards

Freestyle means, above all, being able to do jumps and tricks. This is irrespective of whether it's in the half-pipe or in open terrain.

The set-up of the freestyle board tends to be a soft flex pattern. Stood on its end it reaches up to about chin or tip-of-the-nose height. The shape of its sidecut is medium and generally appears to be on the small side. This allows one to flip from edge to edge more easily, which is particularly important in the half-pipe. You can use a hard binding and soft boots. The step-in system can also be used, but the soft boots should not be too stiff.

Rider: Tanya Baumgartner / Photo: Trauma

Overall length:	Body height minus 20-30 cm
Effective rail length:	Short
Breadth:	Medium
Flex pattern:	Soft
Binding/Boots:	Shell binding/ Step-in binding with soft boots
Angle of binding:	Front 5°-25°/Rear 0°-10°
Use:	Half-pipe/Boarder rink/Piste
Ability:	Advanced/Expert

(Photo: Nitro)

Freeride Boards

The "Freerider" is known for the relaxed fun ride it gives as well as the joy one can have using it in deep snow. The Freerider counts as an allrounder amongst the various snowboards.

The Freeride board is a little less flexible than the Freestyle board and is longer and slightly wider. It should come up to about the tip of your nose. The board is set-up to give good turning ability and absolute edge-of-the-rail riding. Again the preference is to use hard shell and step-in bindings with soft boots.

(Photo: Raichle)

(Photo: Nitro)

Overall length:	Body height minus 20-25 cm
Effective rail length:	Medium
Breadth:	Medium
Flex pattern:	Medium
Binding/Boots:	Shell binding/Step-in binding with soft boots
Angle of binding:	Front 20°-40°/Rear 10°-25°
Use:	Easy to Medium Piste/Cross-country Deep snow
Ability:	Beginner/Expert

SNOW BOARD

Freecarving Boards

When one thinks of freecarving boards, the ambitious, sporting snowboarder springs to mind. They like to make swishing turns, ride cleanly on the edges and traverse down the widest pistes possible. Freecarve boards have therefore a somewhat more sturdy set-up. The board should reach up as far as the nose or up as far as the forehead. Its sidecut is more pronounced than the Freeride board and is generally narrower. Plate bindings with hard boots can be used just as easily as stiff soft boots together with hard shell or step-in bindings.

(Photo: Achim Schmidt)

(Photo: Nitro)

Overall length:	Body height minus 15-20 cm
Effective rail length:	Medium/long
Breadth:	Medium/narrow
Flex pattern:	Medium/hard
Binding/Boots:	Plate bindings with hard boots (also step-in system)/ Shell or step-in bindings with soft boots
Angle of binding:	Front 40º-50º/Rear 2º-8º less
Use:	Medium to demanding piste/Cross-country
Ability:	Advanced/Expert

Race Boards

To be able to come down the piste as fast as possible as if you were carving on rails, or to be able to swish down between the poles when training is what the race board is made for. The race board is hard to very hard. The board reaches up as far as your forehead or a little higher depending on whether you are using it for competition (giant slalom/slalom) or simply for riding on the piste. The slim size of the board and its pronounced sidecut mean that your ride must be exact and exerting. Race boards are not recommended for beginners or even advanced snowboarders. Plate or step-in bindings with hard boots are used exclusively with this type of board.

(Photo: Raichle)

Overall length:	Body height minus 10-15 cm
Effective rail length:	Long
Breadth:	Small
Flex pattern:	Hard
Binding/Boots:	Plate binding with hard boots (also Step-in system with soft boots)
Angle of binding:	Front 45°-60°/Rear 2°-8° less
Use:	Medium to demanding piste
Ability:	Expert/Competition

(Photo: Nitro)

3.2 The Board in Detail
Total length and effective edge length

The measurement of a board is from the tip of the board (called the nose) to the end of the board (called the tail). A short board will begin to 'flutter' more than a longer one at fast speeds. For freestyle and freeriding boards the length should reach up as high as the chin or nose. Freecarve and race boards can easily reach up as high as the forehead.

The total length of the board is always relative to the effective length of the edge. Effective length means the part of the edge of the board, which grips into the snow and thus allows the board to move on the surface.

Hence the following rules: the shorter the effective edge length, the more the board is manoeuvrable. The longer the effective edge length, the greater the turn radius and the smoothness of the ride.

You can easily establish how long the effective edge length is by laying it down on a flat surface. It begins and ends where the edge actually touches the ground.

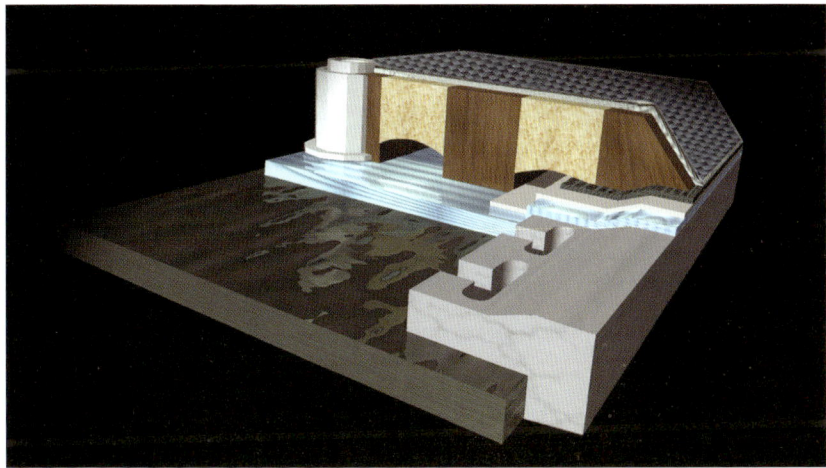

A sectional view of the construction of a board (Graphics: F2)

Breadth and the Sidecut of the Board

Generally, the breadth of the board is measured in three places (at the front, the middle and the rear). Broader boards are particularly suitable for riding in deep snow because they do not sink in so deep. For the freestyle, race and freecarving boards, a narrower board is preferred because they allow better unweighting when executing a change of direction. It is important that the board is not too narrow. The feet should, in any case, not stick out over the sides. The term "sidecut" describes the difference between the narrowest and broadest points along the board. The sidecut is easily worked out by looking at the different measurements of the breadth of the board. Apart from influencing the total length and the effective edge length of the board, the sidecut mainly plays a part in delivering the manoeuvrability of the snowboard. This is expressed generally in the rule: the more the sidecut, the tighter the possible turning moment of the board.

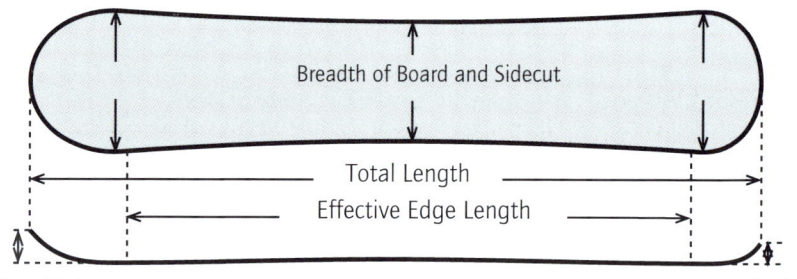

Nose Kick   Tail Kick

Detailed Measurements of the Board (Graphics: Nitro)

The Hardness of the Board

The hardness of the board is adapted to correspond to each type of riding. Race boards and freecarve boards have a hard set-up. They have been designed also for use on hard pistes, having good side-grip and being built for speed. Freestyle and freeride boards, on the other hand, need to have a rather softer set-up. The main thing with them is that they should be able to adapt to the terrain, particularly when jumping and landing or when in the half-pipe.

Flexibility

Flexibility is closely related to the hardness of the board. This means that a specific amount of negative flexibility has to be built into the centre section of the board - this is the area where the bindings are mounted. When the feet bring pressure onto the board, it has to be able to flex so that the whole of the length of the edges on the bottom of the board is pressed down into the snow. When the flexibility is greater, more pressure is needed to bring the board ride under control on its edges.

A high degree of flexibility coupled with a generally hard set-up gives the snowboard dynamic turning characteristics, which means that the board needs to be ridden with a certain amount of aggressiveness and power. Most boards generally tend to have a softer set-up overall. They can be steered with very little effort and are very forgiving to small riding mistakes. This is an important factor to be considered by the beginner or the slightly more advanced when buying a board.

The Rider's Weight

The construction of each snowboard is specifically designed for a particular body weight. The manufacturers give an upper and lower weight limit for each model - watch for this when buying.

Nose and Tail Kick

The nose and tail kick are the way the board lifts up at the front and rear of the board. They influence the effective length of the edges of the board and its riding characteristics. Race and freecarve boards have a slight shovel-type uplift at the front and practically no tail kick. This is because on a hard piste it is important to have the longest edge length possible in order to be able to control the board well. Freestyle boards have relatively greater uplift to enable them to be used for tricks and riding backwards. Sometimes the amount is the same at both the front and the rear. For freeriding boards the kick tends to be long and shaped somewhat flatter so that they do not stick into the snow.

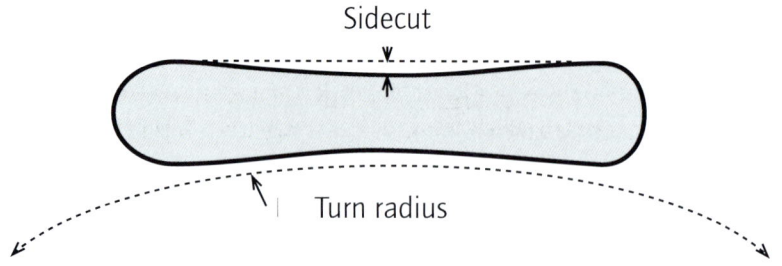

The board's sidecut (Graphics: Nitro)

Tips and Tricks when Buying a Snowboard:
- Does the board match the kind of riding style I wish to adopt?
- Does the board match my body weight?
- Does the board have the correct length and breadth?
- Can I use the board with my choice of boots?

3.3 Bindings and Boots - A Functional Unit

Committing oneself on a particular type of snowboard as well as fulfilling one's own personal wishes is relative to the choice of boot and binding. The rule that every binding is suitable for any board is generally true. There are three types of binding available to the snowboarder: hard shell, plate and step-in bindings. The most important criteria here are freedom of movement, board control and comfort. Snowboarding groups who tend to prefer freedom of movement, like the freestylers or freeriders, use the more comfortable hard shell bindings with soft boots.

The race and carving types, who pay attention to a firm connection with the board and a direct transfer of power, favour the plate binding and hard boots. A relatively new development is the step-in binding. Irrespective of the type of boot, they permit a firm click-connection of the boot into the binding - the same principal as a ski binding being used here for the snowboard. Factors such as simplicity, ease-of-use and comfort make the step-in binding the system of the future. As a general rule, the inserts of each system are screwed onto the board. The inserts are let into the core of the board and thus ensure a firm fixing point. To adjust to the required riding position, the snowboarder can twist-turn them as well as adjust them inwards or outwards. To improve the way the legs stand there is an additional adjustment of placing wedges under the fixing points in order to tip the binding in the desired direction. The rider therefore has a number of adjustment variations to match body weight, ability and riding style.

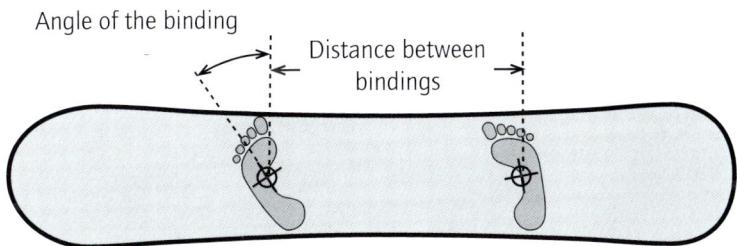

Binding adjustments in detail (Graphics: Nitro)

Suggestions for the distance between bindings

Body size/cm	Distance between bindings/cm
150 – 160	36 – 38
160 – 170	38 – 40
170 – 180	40 – 42
180 – 190	42 – 44

Suggestions for the angle of the binding

Category	Front foot	Rear foot
Beginner	25-35°	5-10° less
Freerider	20-40°	10-25°
Freecarver	40-50°	2-8° less
Racer	45-60°	2-8° less
Freestyler/Half-pipe-rider	5-25°	0-10°

Shell Bindings

Snowboarders, freestylers and freeriders are the main users of these "soft" bindings. They are made up of a base plate, a highback positioned at the rear with two or three padded straps to stabilise the foot and ankle (according to what they are being used for). Because of the open-work plastic construction you are guaranteed freedom of movement.

Hard boots with a plate binding (Photos: Raichle, Nitro)

Soft Boots

To the layman the soft boot looks more like an over-sized hiking boot or snow boot. In effect, it is a lace-up special boot made of waterproof material with a high back and firm sole. Its comfort and imperviousness are excellent. Dependent on where it will be used, the flexibility of the boot varies from being very soft for the freestyler to medium hard for the freerider.

Some models have a removable liner. An individual fit, giving perfect support and increased comfort, can be achieved by using sorbo rubber and a so-called thermoflex system.

Plate Bindings

These solid bindings are targeted mainly towards the freecarver and alpine race groups. The binding consists of a metal base plate, usually on a swivel, and the snowboarding boots are gripped firmly on both edges by its ends. The stable construction affords the rider absolute board control in any situation. Combined with mainly short length boards, the bindings are usually mounted at a slight angle to the direction of movement. Beginners and skiers swapping over to snowboarding have a cheap way out here, in that they can try out their first manoeuvres with their existing ski boots. In the long run, the ski boots should be exchanged for proper special boots for snowboarding.

Hard Boots

The first hard boots were very much like the usual ski touring or downhill ski boots. Because of the particular stresses created by the snowboard, snowboarding boots have been developed with adjustments available at several places, and a built-up shell layered section.

The most important criteria for a comfortable, firm fitting boot are:
- a firm position for the foot and ankle achieved by correctly placed straps
- height of the rear of the boot, the forward lean and the flexibility of the side of the boot all fit the wearer

Just like soft boots, hard boots can be fitted with removable boot liners.

Pair of soft boots and a shell binding (Photos: Raichle, Nitro)

Step-in Bindings

The step-in binding is a recent development, and at the same time, a combination of the two bindings mentioned above. Both hard and soft boots can be used with them by virtue of the clip-in system included. Similar to the click-in systems in cycle racing, metal cleats mounted underneath the sole of the boot click into the fixing mechanism. Having to keep on bending down to do up the clips and metal straps is thing of the past. Because of the differences still existing between systems, boots play a decisive role when deciding what to buy.

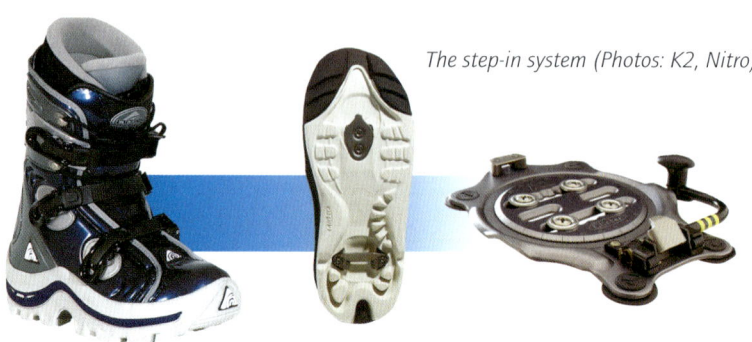

The step-in system (Photos: K2, Nitro)

Step-in Boots

Equipped to accept the step-in system, these boots have the same characteristics as the others above. Alterations can only be made by changing the function of the boot. Incorporating the forward lean adjustment into the boot, for example, compensates for the lack of the highback on the shell binding.

Tips and tricks regarding the binding and the boot

When buying bindings or boots always attempt to try out a combination of the various parts with your snowboard. Check off the details of your personal requirements against our checklist:

- Does the binding fit the board (fitting possibilities/size of the binding relative to the width of the board)?
- Are there sufficient possibilities to adjust the binding (e.g., rotating and centring of the binding)?
- Is the clip system on the binding easy to operate (simple adjustment available and large enough latch)?
- Are the straps well padded?
- Is the relationship between the highback and the height of the soft boot correct? (The shaft of the highback should always be shorter.)
- Does your boot fit in the binding? (Is the shell binding large enough?)
- Check the length of the boot - it should not be longer than the width of the board (hard boots should have a short sole length).
- Is the boot giving sufficient hold on the foot without pressing on it, and do the toes have sufficient movement inside the boot?
- Is the lace-up and latch system user-friendly?
- Is the padding in the boot and on the tongue comfortable?
- Are there pull-up hooks on the tongue and at the back of the shaft?

3.4 Functional 'Clothes Maketh Man'

While snowboarding is now well established, the fashion accompanying it remains just as much 'in' as when it started. Even the conservative skiing fraternity admires the functional, chic fashion worn by the snowboarding freaks. If you want to make sure that you will continue to have fun as you swoop down through the snow, place a little emphasis on having some good clothing. So that you can adapt to the differing weather conditions in the mountains, a warm outfit, consisting of several layers, is recommended. Special material will take care of the wind chill factors and waterproofing without influencing the ability of the body to breathe freely. Additional requisites for the head, arm and leg extremities round off your selection to make a smart outfit. Loose fitting, widely cut articles are an important aid to ensure freedom of movement. Reinforcement of the important parts of the clothing give additional safety and at the same time serves to provide protection against getting wet when landing in the snow.

With so many practical criteria, appearances should not be forgotten since the piste is a kind of 'catwalk' for the winter sports fraternity.

The Outfit

In order to avoid getting wet inside as well as from outside, the best thing to do is to put your clothes on in layers like an onion. Here, in four phases, is a sensible combination of the individual articles of clothing:

SNOW BOARD

Phase 1 - Thermal underwear (Photo: René Marks)

1. In order to strike a good thermal balance between the skin and the clothing, the first layer is a set of thermal underwear separates. Usually, these are made of multi-layered synthetic fibre that permits a healthy perspiration. Dependent on the temperature you can wear either a long sleeved/long legging or short set. In addition a pair of warm sensible socks with a reinforced sole and heel are recommended.

2. Fleecy jumpers are particularly suitable as a second layer. The extremely warm material can be found in various weights and is often offered with wind repellent materials interwoven. Particularly thick versions, with pockets, can actually replace the snowboarding jacket completely.

Phase 2 - The fleecy jumper (Photo: René Marks)

SNOW BOARD

Phase 3 - Details of the snowboard jacket and trousers (Photo: René Marks)

3. The third layer is the one that hits the eye. The jacket and trousers are the showpiece of the snowboarding outfit. The fashion world has already come up with all imaginable variations and colours. The jackets are mainly made of special material and cut long in the arms and at the back. On top of this there are reinforcements, fasteners on the sleeve ends and at the collar, as well as ventilation slits. All these points have become convention. It serves well on cold days to have a removable hood as well as a high collar.

The all-rounder amongst the snowboarding jackets is a combination of a light functional jacket with a removable fleece lining. This makes adapting to the temperature simple.

The material used for snowboarding trousers differs little from that for the jacket. On those parts where there is a lot of wear and contact with the snow is unavoidable - the seat and the knee areas - there is additional reinforcement.

The imperviousness of the bottom of the trousers is also very important. A loose fitting garment with a high backed rear to the trousers, held up by bracers, is a guarantee that even in low temperatures you will continue to have fun.

Useful Accessories

4. This fourth phase is devoted to accessories. Gloves are the most important ones. There are various forms in the range, from the thin, tight-fitting gloves to warm 'fist-full' ones - all kinds are available. As a good compromise there are gloves with only two fingers. The forefinger and the middle finger fit together in one and the ring finger and the little finger in the other. They are really warm and still leave enough feeling to allow you to open the binding latches. Long gloves with adjustable fasteners, as well as reinforcements at all the important places, are now standard. Removable linings permit articles to be dried quickly ready for the next day. To protect the wrists there are pre-formed plastic shapes that are fitted into the gloves. A good idea to have - not just only for beginners.

Apart from gloves, a hat is something that must belong to every snowboarder's outfit. They keep the head warm and at the same time give protection from the strong rays of the sun. A firm seat of the trousers and use of quality material are also important. Fleece material and synthetic fibres offer a good compromise and balance between insulation and perspiration.

Phase 4 - Accessories (Photos: adidas, K2, Nitro, Swatch)

Talking about the sun, you should always think of having either snow goggles or sunglasses. Being on a glacier wearing a good pair of glasses, capable of filtering out the extremely strong ultra-violet rays, is very important. The choice of the type of glasses has to be left up to personal individual preferences. Snowboarders however should concentrate more on the requirement for snow goggles because the technical characteristics are better. They have a ventilation system, all-round protection against the sun, changeable lenses and sit well, having an adjustable elasticised strap to give the rider safety when riding. Otherwise modern sports glasses offer the best compromise between function and optics. Equipped with the features of their 'big brothers', the snow goggles can still make a show on the beach promenade. They lie close to the shape of the head on the sides, giving protection against the wind and the rays of the sun.

Sports glasses - good looking and versatile (Photo: adidas)

The group of accessories that are not absolutely necessary, but really quite useful, is made up of those items that make the life of the snowboarder a little easier - these are things like board bags, rucksacks and watches, amongst others.

One of the watches, which is very effective even though it's tucked away under the snow jacket, is called "Swatch Access" and is being used at more than 300 skiing stations in over 30 countries. The snowboarder simply casually lifts his arm and the barrier on the ski lift lifts automatically. Recently, there is also a wrist-speedometer on the market for those snowboarders who have ambitions to go fast. Ciclosport HAC-Watches give the altitude, elapsed time and an approximate board speed.

Tips and Tricks:
- Various clothing articles and accessories can be adapted from other types of sport (special underwear, fleecy jumpers, sports goggles and glasses).
- Special material (e.g., Gore-Tex and Sympatex) must be treated from time to time with the prescribed impregnating agent.

SNOWBOARD

40

Everything's possible...(Photo: Raichle)

4 STARTING SNOWBOARDING - LET'S GO!

As we know, snowboarding is a relatively recent type of sport and so, accordingly, one finds that most of the snowboarders come from the youth sector. Gradually there are signs of an increase of grown-ups venturing to take up snowboarding when on holiday. While young people simply go straight into snowboarding, most of the adults come across from skiing and make their first daring attempts on test runs.

There are several different opinions on how best to start. At the beginning, skiers will find the standing position, with the fixed leg, a little unusual and difficult. On the other hand they come from skiing with the advantage of having already gained a 'feeling' for the snow when gliding and carving.

In order to make a satisfactory start it is recommended that candidates from both these groups visit a snowboarding school. Without undergoing systematic learning and getting to know the various tips, any start in this fascinating type of sport becomes unnecessarily difficult.

Using a system of trial and error, you will be waiting a very long time for your first successes. Because, unlike in skiing, there are different snowboarding binding systems (soft and hard), at the beginning it is advisable to hire an outfit, so that after a few days you can try out the other system. It is easier to start off with hard boots and a plate binding.

After you have done the first few learning steps under the eye of a snowboarding instructor, you will be able to improve your ability by putting in enough practice and by watching others and copying them. For advanced students there is also nothing wrong with attending a snowboarding course. In the following chapter, we cover an overview of practical lessons in snowboarding instruction, and at the same time it serves as an aid for those who want to go at it alone and use the 'do-it-yourself' system.

4.1 First Steps with the Board

Gathering experience regarding the different body movements as well as learning to keep your balance are items that are the first priority for the snowboarding student. But before we get going you have to find out which way to stand on the board.

From the Standing Position to Roller Skating -
"Regular" or "Goofy"

The terms "regular" and "goofy" describe the two different ways of standing on the board. The descriptions come from wave surfing and skateboarding and have been taken on by snowboarders. The "regular" stands on the board with the left foot in the leading binding, while the "goofy" has the right foot forward. Before starting out to gain your first experiences, you have to establish which foot you put in the leading binding. There are various different ways of finding out what your correct foot position is.

Tips and Tricks:
- If you fall forward with your eyes closed, which foot do you lead off with? This test can be done with a partner, who gives you a little push forward (see Figure 1).
- Just imagine you are a boxer. Adopt the boxing position. Which of your feet is forward? (see Figure 1)
- Which of your feet is forward when you slide forward on some ice or snow?
- When you stand up from doing a press-up, which foot do you lift off the ground first?

SNOW BOARD

Figure 1 a: "Goofy" or "Regular" - shadow boxing (Photo: René Marks)

Figure 1 b: "Goofy" or "Regular" - the push (Photo: René Marks)

Carrying and Laying Down the Board

When carrying the board in the crowd at the ski lift station you should take care not to create a danger to anyone else. You should therefore carry the board vertically and close to the body. Additionally there should be a safety leash attached and fastened around the wrist.

Again, when you put the board down, always think of safety. A wayward board, without an owner, can be a danger to all the other winter sportsmen. This is why you always lay the board down on the piste with the bindings facing down into the snow (see Figure 2).

When stopping off at a ski or snowboard hut it is always recommended that you attach the board by its leash to a ski stand to avoid it slipping away or falling down.

Figure 2: Carrying and laying down the board (Photo: René Marks)

Strapping onto the Board

You can strap on the snowboard in either the sitting or standing position. Which of these two variants you use rather depends on the steepness of the slope as well as your ability.

Generally, the rule applies that the steeper the slope the more difficult it is to strap the board on in the standing position. Always strap the forward foot into the binding first and then the rear foot. The safety leash is fixed to the forward foot first in order to avoid the board inadvertently slipping away.

When getting into the bindings, the board should face across the fall-line and the boots as well as the bindings should be cleared of snow. The simplest way of getting into the bindings on a slope is to combine standing with your back facing downhill and then strapping down your front foot. The rear foot is placed under the board to hold it. Finally, sitting down with your back to the slope, the rear foot is fixed into the binding.

A substantial innovation, and at the same time a simplification of getting into the bindings, is the new step-in system. For the snowboarder they allow a child's play way of putting the bindings on (see Figure 3).

Figure 3: Strapping on the board (Photo: Achim Schmidt)

Falling Down and Getting Up

Should it come to a crash, it is possible to avoid injury by carrying out a controlled way of falling down. Everyone must get to learn this technique and allow enough time to practice it thoroughly. Learning the controlled fall helps to break down any fears of a crash out and it prepares the snowboarder for such an eventuality. For beginners the controlled fall can be used as an emergency brake - just in case all other forms of braking have no effect. It is less dangerous to let yourself fall at low speed than to crash out uncontrolled at high speed. There are different techniques for a fall to the frontside and the backside, which can be learned and practised with and without the snowboard.

Falling Frontside

The starting position for both types of fall is almost identical. The legs are bent and the body is lowered down. The arms are held out in front of the body and are slightly bent. From this starting position the frontside fall is carried out by falling stretched out flat onto the snow similar to a volleyball player jack-knifing after a low shot (see Figure 4). The weight of the fall is taken mainly on the lower arms. The hands should not be used to check the fall as there is a good chance of damaging the wrist joints this way.

Falling Backside

For the backside fall, first of all you take up the same starting position as described above, but this time with the arms lying more to the side of the body. Then you slowly let yourself fall backwards rolling over on your back. The chin is pressed down onto the chest so that the head doesn't hit the ground as you fall (see Figure 5). The arms alongside the body help to cushion the fall. You shouldn't stretch out your arms to brake the fall.

SNOW BOARD

47

Figure 4: Falling frontside (Photo: René Marks)

Figure 5: Falling backside (Photo: René Marks)

Standing Up

In the beginning, standing up will feel somewhat unusual, because of the fact that the bindings are fixed. It therefore requires practise. Before standing up the board should be placed at right angles to the fall of the slope.

If this is not done then the board will slip down the slope and with it the rider on free fall for a short period of time. To stand up you simply change the centre of balance of the body by slipping your bottom down towards the board. You then position your forward hand in the snow near to the nose of the snowboard (see Figure 6).

You then give a good shove off with your hand, and by swinging the centre of balance forwards you stand up over the forward leg. It is easier to get into the standing position when the slope is steeper. If difficulty is experienced trying to stand up from the backside edge, the board can be switched over to the frontside while still lying down (see Figure 7). Standing up from the frontside works on the same principle and is relatively easier.

Switching Over the Board While Still in the Bindings

As we have just shown in the previous paragraph, it is easier for the beginner to stand up from the frontside edge. You therefore need to be able to do a switch over of the board from the backside to the frontside while it is still strapped on.

First of all, while still lying down, lift the board off the snow and put it onto its tail. To be able to do this you need to have strong back muscles - you can get assistance from a partner when trying it out for the first few times. You then turn onto your stomach over the fulcrum of the raised board. The board follows the movement of the body and you end up on the frontside edge (see Figure 7).

SNOW BOARD

49

Figure 6: Standing up (Photo: René Marks)

Figure 7: Switching over the board while still in the bindings (Photo: Achim Schmidt)

SNOW BOARD

50

(Photo: René Marks)

Skating

Skating is the first opportunity for the snowboarder to have the feeling of moving forward under his own power. The beginner gets the experience of gliding along on the snowboard. Besides this, being able to skate properly is an important requirement for getting in and out of the ski lift chair or T-bar. Basically you skate along just like you did as a child on your scooter down the road.

When skating along with the snowboard, only the forward foot is firmly fixed in the binding. In order to gain impetus one pushes off (like paddling) with the rear foot, and during the glide, you put the foot onto the anti-slip pad between the bindings (see Figure 8).

With a little practise you can repeat the paddling movement and glide along for some way. The snowboarder should look straight ahead and not down at the board.

Figure 8: Skating on the snowboard (Photos: Achim Schmidt)

Care must be taken to ensure that the clamps on the rear binding are folded over onto the inside of the board and do not hang over the edges, dragging in the snow and creating a brake.

Although it appears to be a simple action, care must be taken as the board is fixed to the forward foot. On the one hand this gives the beginner ample chance to get used to the standing position on the board. On the other hand you must not underestimate the strain and leverage placed on the knee joint. Subsequently skating should only be done on flat terrain and never downhill at speed.

4.2 Basic Exercises on the Board
From the Basic Position to Diagonal Running

The definition of "basic position" is the position of 'standing' that all snowboarders adopt before setting off for a ride. The ankle, knee and hip joints are slightly bent. The weight of the body is evenly distributed over both feet and the arms are slightly bent in front of the body (see Figure 9).

From this basic position you can move off in all directions. Therefore, this position is called the "ready" position. By taking deep breaths and rocking up and down on the board after adopting the standing position, this allows the beginner to find a relaxed and comfortable position before moving off, ready for any action he wants to take on.

Figure 9: The basic position (Photo: Achim Schmidt)

Jumping and Hopping

Jumping with the board strapped to your feet trains the snowboarder's balance and steadiness. From the basic position that we have just learned about, the centre of balance of the body is slightly lowered by bending the knees a little. From this position you do the jump by pushing off sharply with the legs (see Figure 10).

On landing, the body's joints give a little to soften any shock. After each jump the body adopts the neutral ready position in order to set yourself up again for the next movement.

By twisting the upper body during the jump you can turn the direction of the board in the air. Executing several of these mid-air twist jumps, the snowboarder can turn through 360° and thus draw a kind of flower outline in the snow.

Figure 10: Jumping (Photos: René Marks)

Gliding and Schussing

Schussing gives the snowboarder his first experience of gliding on the board with both feet firmly fixed in the bindings. The jump should be practised on a slight slope with a suitable run-out stretch or an uphill section at the end of it so that the speed is slowed down. You glide along with the board in a flat position. The weight of the body is positioned over the forward foot and the nose of the board points in a downhill direction. The snowboarder keeps his eyes on the direction of movement (see Figure 11).

Gliding and schussing teaches the snowboarder how to keep the board in the desired direction without tipping over or slipping away sideways. Being able to go straight is important when using the ski-lift. The feeling of gliding can also be experienced on flat ground by getting a partner to push or pull you along.

Figure 11: Gliding (Photo: Achim Schmidt)

Canting, Sliding and Braking

Canting the snowboard is one of the essential requirements to be able to do all the turn movements and to be able to brake. The initial canting exercises deal with balance and practise to get used to doing it. It requires gentle, gradual movements of the ankle, knee and hip joints so that the board does not jerk. The ground should not be too flat, otherwise when the board is placed flat on the ground, the danger of canting is present and there is a danger of slipping downhill. A crash out like that is very much more unpleasant than falling into the slope. In order to achieve a gradual braking, the snowboarder tries to put the board first flat and then on its edges alternately and rhythmically (see Figure 12).

Your weight is distributed evenly on both feet and the board is at right angles to the fall line. So that you are able to negotiate a simple piste before you are able to turn, it will be important to perfect canting, both on the frontside as well as the backside.

Figure 12: Canting and sliding (Photos: Achim Schmidt)

The first few exercises at canting can be carried out using a partner so that you are able to keep your balance. As soon as you have managed to get a feeling of security and can keep your balance during your canting and slipping exercises, you can carry out further practice on your own and put the first few metres behind you.

Tips and Tricks:
- When bending the legs to cant on the frontside or to slip on the backside, the toes are pressed down onto the sole of the boots.
- When stretching the legs to slip on the frontside or to cant on the backside the toes are pulled up as if one was running on the heels.

Moving Diagonally

Moving diagonally is one step further on from the slip movement. As you slip you transfer the weight of the body onto the forward leg. The nose of the board tends to drop downhill and it begins to drift diagonally forwards and downhill on the edge of the board. Gradually applying this canting technique, by using the toe and heel pressure already described above, you bend and lift the legs to give yourself good speed control. Your eyes are fixed on the point you want to reach and not down at your own feet. Using the diagonal technique on the frontside and the backside, you can now reach points lying on the left and right of the piste for the first time.

The first change of direction movements were done by laying down and switching the board over. Now with the diagonal technique you can move off in the other direction. Gradually gaining confidence and using the canting method, the snowboarder can try to vary his speed. The gliding phase - when the board moves flat over the snow more rapidly - will automatically get longer. With even more practice, the snowboarder will be able to apply yet more edge when canting. The ability to brake as well as self-confidence grows step by step.

SNOW BOARD

In free flight – Guillaume Chastagnol (Photo: Skye Chalmers)

Riding the Lift

Climbing up the slope for the first few times with all your equipment can be a very strenuous business. In order to make learning a little easier for the beginner, the technique of using the lift is introduced at an early stage. The previous experience necessary for this has already been achieved by roller skating and gliding.

A short ride on a T-bar lift on a nursery slope is a good way to learn how to use it. The time sitting on the lift serves as a well earned break after the downhill run. Using the lift is a considerable aid to getting up the hill and for all snowboarders quite a sense of achievement.

Initially using the ski-lift is an unusual experience. Usually you will need several attempts to successfully complete the whole lift stretch in one go. But even a short lift up is quite a thrill. Should you come to grief on the lift you must clear the slip-way as quickly as possible so that you don't place the other lift users at danger.

Lifts on nursery slopes move slower than others so that getting on and off is easier. You can also let the lift personnel know that you need some assistance when getting on. Lifts can be either ones with a T-bar or with a chair, although the principles of how they work are the same. Unlike the T-bar lift, in the chair lift you can only go on your own.

It is better for the beginner to try out the first few lift journeys together with an experienced skier or snowboarder, who can hold on to him and provide a safety factor. The goofy rider should use the right hand lane while the regular rider uses the left hand lane. This is so that, in either case, the lift bar can be held onto firmly in front of the body. When getting onto the lift the board must be placed in the direction of movement and the rear foot placed alongside and outside of the board. The T-bar piece or the plate seat is hooked in behind the thighs and the rear foot is placed between the bindings on the anti-slip pad for safety (see Figure 13). As with all other occasions, you keep your eyes in the direction of movement. When getting off the lift you take the T-pole from behind the legs and then let go of it. You must leave the dismount area quickly, so that you don't get in the way of other lift users and endanger them. The paddle-glide that you have been practising earlier will help here.

Figure 13: Getting on the ski-lift (Photo: Achim Schmidt)

The beginner usually has no idea really on how to react when using the ski-lift. Because of this you can simulate the lift by using an old T-pole or a ski stick. When you practise it will soon be clear that you don't actually sit on the T-bar itself, but let yourself be pulled along in a slightly bent standing position.

4.3 Snowboarding Technique I - The First Downhill Attempt
The Various Basic Turn Movements

The turn is the way you make the first deliberate change of direction and is one of the basic skills of snowboarding. Essentially, snowboarding is for most a purely recreation sport. Thus, sticking to too many hard and fast rules hinders the sportsman rather than help him. The student is helped more by giving him just an idea of how to do a particular exercise. Thus the instruction given by the trainer does not necessarily have to have any particular or specific pre-set solution or aim. On the contrary, it's the fun and the freedom of any individual's style that is more important. As a result the technique that has to be imparted is the one that gives the greatest degree of progress according to ability. Here we are talking about the drift turn by using the body.

Figure 14: Drift turn backside (Photos: René Marks)

The Basic Drift Turn (With the Body Twist)

The basic turn movements are done using the drift turn on a flat prepared piste area (see Figures 14 and 15). The turn is done by twisting the upper-body in the desired direction, at the same time canting the board. The upper-body twists against the legs. As this movement is transmitted into the legs and with the weight of the body on the forward leg, the board, laid flat on the surface, follows the direction in which the upper body has twisted. Changing the weight over to the new direction, the board is finally edged over and drifts round on the inside edge of the turn.

Speed and the amount you twist your body to start the swing has a direct influence on the radius of the turn. Moving into a drift turn is made easier the faster and the more the body is twisted.

Figure 15: Drift turn frontside (Photos: René Marks)

Tips and Tricks:
- For the beginner, being able to get across the fall line of the slope and then move diagonally across it, is the most important aim. If you spend too long going downhill at the beginning, you will pick up too much speed and this will lead to panicking.
- Twisting your body and hips early enough is a prerequisite for a clean speedy drift turn.
- Repeating the rotation of the upper body must not be carried out until the first turn has been completed otherwise the impulse of the turn will not be transferred to the legs.
- By moving the weight onto the forward leg before going into the turn, the board is unweighted at the tail and will be able to move round freely.

4.4 Snowboarding Technique II - Advanced Manoeuvres
Turns Using the Unweighting System
The Unweighted Edge Turn

The essential characteristic of this type of turn is the phase of unweighting the board and gradually applying a bending movement, pressing down with the legs as you steer into the turn. Unlike the drift turn, the edge turn is executed as far as possible on the edge of the board. The drifting element is missed out and the board scribes the semicircular direction chosen, dependant on the sidecut of the board. As it does you will be able to see a characteristic, clear line cut in the snow. In order to carry out this technique, a little faster speed is called for and you need to lean more into the turn. The aim is for the beginner to be able to string several turns together rhythmically so that they practically melt into one movement.

It is easier for the snowboarder to do the basic turn with hard boots on than with soft boots. Because of the stiff shell form of the hard boots, there is more direct, and thus optimum, transfer of force onto the board. Soft boots tend to be relatively softer and more flexible. They give the snowboarder more freedom of movement on the board, but, by virtue of the indirect transfer of force on the board, they rather give the impression of a spongy ride.

The unweighted edge turn can be divided up into four phases (see Figures 16 & 17 on the following double page).

Start/Preparation
- With the body in the central position, prepare for the turn from the traverse. The weight of the body is distributed equally on both legs.

Moving into the turn
- As you move into the turn you push up using the ankle, knee and hip joints. The upward push into the change of direction is done forwards and downhill. You shift your weight on to the forward foot. Simultaneously, as your weight shifts on the upward movement, you tip the board onto its edge.

Steering
- By actively and gradually pushing down with your body and pumping the legs the board edge grips into the snow. The board is edged more by leaning more into the turn. In order to achieve optimum balance, your weight is distributed on both legs as you steer into the turn.

End of the turn/Preparation
- Because each of the turns should flow into one movement, the end of the turn is, at the same time, the preparatory phase for the next turn. From the bent stance as you steer, you assume the central position again and gradually ease off the edges.

SNOW BOARD

64

Figure 16: The edge turn with unweighted backside (Photos: René Marks)

SNOWBOARD

Figure 17: The edge turn with unweighted frontside (Photos: René Marks)

Tips and Tricks:

- If the unweighting phase is not carried out effectively enough and as a result edging is made difficult, the turn can be carried out by jumping. The board can be "jumped" over the fall line. During the jump the board can be turned into the new direction in the air.

- The upper body should not be twisted against the direction of movement during the turn. As an aid, just imagine you are carrying a full tray of drinks in the hand on the outside of the curve. In this way your torso will turned in the direction of the ride as you go round the curve.

- Another tip is to imagine that at the beginning of the turn you are picking up a box on the outside of the curve and setting it down again at the end of the turn. Besides giving you an improved body stance it will assist you with the unweighting movement.

The Weighted Edge Turn

Turning by applying the weight downwards serves to prepare the snowboarder for riding in deep snow and on mogul terrain. Mastering the weighted edge turn is also a great help in bumpy and hilly terrain. Since the beginner will rarely find himself in such terrain at the beginning, this technique does not need to be learned early on, unlike the turns already mentioned which are 'musts'. However, the snowboarder who wants to get through all types of terrain must learn how to master the technique of using weighted movements. Before you go off in open terrain, choose a flat, prepared piste area with plenty of space to practise first.

The sequence of movements for the turn with the weighting technique is exactly the opposite to the turn with the unweighting method. By pressing down sharply on the board with the legs at the start of the turn, the board will be unweighted. By then gradually pumping the whole body upwards, you steer through the curve. It is particularly important to keep on stretching up with the legs, using a well-timed and constant rhythm right up to the end of the turn. This is the only way to be sure of an optimum steering movement. If your legs are already stretched right up before the end of the turn, the radius of the curve can only be corrected by leaning the body well into the turn, and then precise steering is not possible any more.

If the weighted turns go well on a prepared piste you can then try them out on different types of terrain. On bumpy terrain or on moguls the weighted turn is ridden as a so-called "balancing" movement. The bumps are simply "swallowed up" as you ride over them. You don't need to actively bend your legs - they have to work more like a shock absorber as they meet the bump. In the bent riding stance the turn starts as you hit the bump. Steering is achieved as you ride over the bump while at the same time extending the legs in the direction of the hollow and edging the board. The aim is not to be thrown up by the bump or mogul during the ride. On the contrary, you should try to suppress the up and down movement caused by the bumpy terrain and maintain contact with the snow. This is the only way to have a controlled ride.

Figure 18: The weighted turn backside. (Photos: René Marks)

Figure 19: The weighted turn frontside (Photos: René Marks)

The weighted turn is also used when riding in deep snow. By suddenly relaxing the muscles as you turn, you effect an unweighting movement (passive squatting). The board is lifted up and practically 'swims' momentarily on top of the powder snow.

By shifting the centre of balance of your upper body, the board can be turned in the new direction. With a gradual application of pressure using the legs, the board can be brought onto its edge ready for the next turn. The weighted turn is also done in four phases (see Figures 18 & 19).

Start/Preparation
- You start from the traverse slipping motion with your body slightly upright. The weight of the body is distributed equally on both legs.

Moving into the turn
- As you move into the turn you push down quickly using the ankle, knee and hip joints. The downward push, just like the push up for unweighting, is done forwards and downhill into the change of direction. You shift your weight onto the forward foot. Simultaneously, as your weight shifts on the downwards movement, you tip the board onto its edge.

Steering
- As you lean into the curve, the edge of the board bites into the snow. At the same time, you actively and gradually stretch the legs up as you go through the steering phase. With more speed, and by pulling in more, the radius of the turn can be increased. In order to achieve optimum balance, your weight is distributed on both legs as you steer into the turn.

End of the turn/Preparation
- Just like the unweighting technique, each of the turns should flow as far as possible into one movement. From the stretched up position at the end of the turn you assume the central position again and gradually ease off the edges.

Tips and Tricks:
- Unweighting will be greater the faster you carry out the bending movement as you start the turn. As a result it will be easier to turn the board in the new direction. A complete unweighting situation will be possible if you let yourself drop momentarily. Pushing down slowly, on the other hand, is aimed to produce less unweighting.

4.5 Workshop - Easier Snowboarding
Learning Using Variations

As we said in the last section, it is not necessary that the absolute perfect technique is mastered, and indeed, this is not really the aim for most snowboarders.

It is more a question of having fun with the snowboard on the piste, and this moment will come as soon as you have experienced the first few successes. In this respect, the right way of riding is more a means to the end.

By systematically going through the introductory phases and taking note of the right tips at the right time, the learning process for the beginner will be accelerated and simplified.

After the first few turns have been done and you have not only gained a certain amount of feeling for the way the board behaves, but also started to develop your own movements, then by watching other snowboarders and copying them you will pick up even more knowledge.

Also a special course at a snowboard school will help you to develop your own personal style of riding further. This will train you in the various different actions that make up a swing turn rather than look at the swing turns as a single flowing movement.

By examining the various aspects and characteristics of the turn, the snowboarder will be able to put himself in a situation where he will be able to react appropriately to every differing set of circumstances that he will meet in different terrain, and in so doing, perfect his style.

The actions, together with their respective variations and exercises, that come into question are:

The twist of the body when starting the turn (anticipating the turn)

Variations:

- Turning the body slowly/quickly
- Turning the body a lot/a little

Exercises:

- Standing on top of a mound of snow, turn the body quickly into another direction. The board will follow and point in the new direction
- Jump up in the air on flat ground and whilst in the air twist the body in a new direction. On landing the board will automatically be pointing in the new direction
- Going down a slight slope try to do the exercises just described

Stretching and bending movements (Verticals) when starting the turn and steering

Variations:

- Stretching/Bending movement slowly and gradually applied
- Stretching/Bending movement applied quickly and explosively
- Stretching/Bending movement applied only a little or completely

Exercises:

- Swing turn with a jump onto the edges
- Turning without a vertical movement
- Deliberately ride in a low or high position

SNOW BOARD

The optimum basic position (Photo: Raichle)

An extreme rearward leaning position in deep snow (Photo: Raichle)

Placing your weight over either the tip or the tail of the board

Variations:

- When starting the turn place the weight over the front leg
- When steering in the turn, distribute your weight evenly over both legs
- At the end of the turn place your weight over the rear leg

Exercises:

- Standing, place your weight forwards and backwards until the board starts to lift up from the snow at the ends
- Leaning well forward or backwards, ride along turning as you go
- Ride along without changing your position forwards or backwards (central position) and do turns like this
- Go along deliberately putting your weight either onto the rear or forward foot like a pendulum as you turn

The stance in the turn and canting

The various different ways of holding yourself and canting depend very much on the speed of the snowboard. If you lean too much into the turn at low speed you will find yourself lying in the snow again.

However, the opposite is not possible. It is not possible to do a high speed turn without leaning well into it in the first place. Just think of the comparison of a motorbike or bicycle rider.

Variations:

- Doing turns with differing radii at the same speed as far as possible
- Leaning into the turn at different degrees at the same speed
- Gradually increasing your speed and your lean into the turn

Exercises:

- Go into a turn with relatively high speed and lean into it like a motorbike rider. Let the board run through the turn and steer out of it, gliding until you come to a standstill
- As above, except that at the end of the turn carry out an upwards vertical movement trying to get off the snow and start to begin the next turn
- Without laying your body steeply into the turn, use your knees and hips to steer through the turn. You can deliberately change each of these actions - each one will have a different influence on the turn you are making. For example a turn can be ridden with more or less upper body twist, or alternatively the twist of the body follows slower or quicker. In exactly the same way there will be a difference if you do the stretch up as you enter the turn slowly or quickly

The variations and exercises described should help the snowboarder to be able to put his experiences and the reactions he has learned into practice as well as to learn what his board will do in certain circumstances. After a few snowboarding holidays, and by having as many of these various experiences behind you, you will be in a position to master any extremely difficult situation that you might meet.

(Photo: René Marks)

4.6 Suitable Equipment for Better Snowboarding

Mistakes which crop up are not necessarily due to bad techniques. After the usual business of getting used to things and being able to do things automatically, even the slightly advanced snowboarder will be able to detect the difference between various boards and their characteristics. Being able to try out different types of boards (friends and acquaintances/snowboard hire/test centres etc.) is a useful aid to choosing a new board.

Only by personally trying out the board can you ascertain its suitability for your particular style of riding. You should be quite prepared, and not surprised, that a board you haven't used before will have completely different characteristics to what you are used to. Therefore it is recommended that you take it easy with a new board. This is particularly so for those coming across from skiing or who have changed over from soft to hard boots and the associated binding systems or vice versa.

In practice this all means one thing for the snowboarder: mistakes, particularly those that you repeatedly make, can also be down to having the wrong equipment.

The board is too wide!

The toes and the heels must never stick out over the side of the board. On the other hand, riders with small shoe sizes can have a problem by having their toes or heels too far away from the edge of the board. Such cases will find it more difficult to transfer power on to the edge and this will disadvantage their manoeuvrability.

The board is too hard and inflexible!

Because the board is too inflexible it will not grip into the snow along the complete effective length of its edge - rather only at the front and the rear areas. The board scrapes over the surface of the snow as a result and there is no control on the edges.

The board is too flexible!

If the board is too soft - could be that it is not suitable to carry the weight of the rider - the pressure applied by the rider will not be stable and the front of the board will dig into the snow.

The binding is not properly mounted on the board!

a) The distance between bindings is too little.

Too short a distance between the bindings results in a bad stance and influences one's balance, leading to crashes.

b) The distance between bindings is too big.

If the bindings are mounted too far apart, the snowboarder will be placed in an anatomically poor stance. Because they are fixed, when a riding mistake is made, it can easily lead to applying pressure wrongly and thus ending up with knee injuries. Besides this, your balance will be affected when standing. Suggestions for the distance between bindings are:

Body Height/cm	Distance between bindings/cm
150 – 160	36 – 38
160 – 170	38 – 40
170 – 180	40 – 42
180 – 190	42 – 44

c) The angular difference between the front and rear bindings is too small, or the angle at which the bindings are mounted is too steep.

If the binding is angled too steeply it allows very little application of pressure on the edges of the board. When the angle of the binding is about right and there is less of an angle on the rear foot binding, more pressure can be applied and this makes manoeuvrability easier. Your balance when standing is also improved. Suggestions for the best binding angle are (see page 29):

Category	Front foot	Rear foot
Beginner	25-35°	5-10° less
Freerider	20-40°	10-25°
Freecarver	40-50°	2- 8° less
Racer	45-60°	2- 8° less
Freestyler/ Half-pipe-rider	5-25°	0-10°

SNOW BOARD

80

...and the winner is...Charlotte Bernard / World Champion Duel, 1997 (Photo: Wojciech)

5 SPORTS, ACTION & FUN
5.1 Competitive Snowboarding

The time has long gone when competitive snowboarding was only done by a small band of enthusiasts. The image of the cool snowboarder who does a couple of races or so, just for fun, has changed to one of a totally dedicated, well-trained professional. Since the creation of the first World Cup Races and the inauguration of snowboarding into the Winter Olympic programme, the sport has developed rapidly.

In the meantime, the larger snowboarding manufacturers, as well as sponsors from completely other interests, are there with their top teams competing in all the large snowboarding events looking for business. Modern training methods and a full programme guarantee well trained competitors, who are out there fighting for every tenth of a second on the piste or for the last centimetre in the half-pipe. Interviews, photo calls and fan mail have become everyday items for a lot of the top sportsmen and women. Those who haven't quite made it yet are working hard for a place at the top.

But, despite all this, the sport has managed to maintain a little of its flair. The very distinct feeling of joy, exuded by the snowboarder, is felt by the spectator at each of the large events. On the sidelines of the sport a whole programme has been established with live music, parties, attractions and a hint of a 'happy-go-lucky' feeling that grips everyone - a party for the sake of a party, so to speak.

The competitions are divided into three categories, namely race, freestyle and freeride. These stem from skiing and, over the course of time, have been developed further for snowboarding as well as to produce an effect as a spectator sport. By making the courses short and using a parallel start, variations have been developed so that two competitors race against each other in an exciting battle. The freestyle artists have 'borrowed' their course styles from the skateboarding and BMX camps. All possible types of jumps and manoeuvres are run in the half-pipe and a jury marks the runs according to certain criteria. With a lot of creativity, which can be followed by the spectators close up, this latter type of competition is one of the favourites in the snowboarding scene. In addition to the race events, the half-pipe competition has now been rewarded by being included in the Olympic programme.

Training in the Half-pipe (Photo: Raichle)

Boardercross - a freeride style - is an event that has been 'home-grown' by the snowboarders. This is where competition 'meets' fun for the snowboarder again. It is a course with various different types of terrain, obstacles and jumps as a challenge to the all-rounder amongst competitors. Up to six "gladiators" compete against each other as they race off round the course, giving the spectators a good show. Whatever the preference or ambition each snowboarder has, there is something suitable for him in competitive snowboarding.

It's all about fun - snowboard professionals Fabien Rohrer and Max Plotzeneder (Photo: Nitro)

In snowboarding camps, which specialise on the competitive side of the sport, you can gain your first experiences, tips and a direct comparison with others under the watchful eye of professionals. National associations (see Pages 163 and 165 for web pages and addresses) can give you information about the race event programme and entry conditions. So? - There's absolutely nothing standing in your way to get into the racing scene.

Racing
Giant Slalom (GS)

The giant slalom has been adopted from skiing and is the speed event in the racing branch. The rider tries to jink through the widely spread gates, on the edges, as dynamically as possible at top speed. The prerequisites to finding the optimum speed line lie in a perfect control of your body, polished riding techniques and perfectly tuned race equipment. Because of the length of the course and the high speeds reached, this event provides the greatest challenge to both rider and equipment.

The Giant Slalom (Rider: Simon Schoch / Photo: Wojciech)

SNOWBOARD

In Nagano, in 1998, the giant slalom was included in the Winter Olympics. Each competition consists of two timed runs. The fastest riders from the first run qualify for the final, from which the winner emerges.

Technical Data - Giant Slalom (Averages)

Length:	approximately 800-1,200 m
Breadth:	at least 20 m
Altitude Difference:	at least 180 m
Number of gates:	10-13% the altitude difference
Distance between gates:	about 20 m

Parallel Slalom (Duel (DU))

Compared with the giant slalom, the parallel slalom is carried out on a much shorter course where the gates are placed much closer together. The challenge to the rider is therefore placed more on his sense of co-ordination, reaction and his riding technique.

In this face to face - rider against rider - confrontation, the psychological factor and the knockout system employed play an important role. Qualification for the parallel slalom takes place in a run where the fastest 32 riders are decided. Following this there are two runs where the competitors run parallel against each other to come up with the last 16 runners for the knockout system.

The final rounds are run as quarter-finals, semi-finals and a final.

Parallel Slalom - Karl-Heinz Zangerl in action (Photo: Wojciech)

Parallel Giant Slalom

In the parallel giant slalom, the characteristics of the parallel slalom and the giant slalom are combined - with great effect for the spectating public. Just as in the parallel slalom two riders start together against each other.

The distance between gates is, however, increased considerably and resembles more the conditions of the fast ride in the downhill style of the giant slalom.

SNOW BOARD

Technical Data - Slalom (Averages)

Length:	approximately 300 m
Width:	at least 20 m
Altitude Difference:	at least 80 m
Number of gates:	20-25
Distance between gates-Slalom:	10-15 m
Distance between gates-Giant Slalom:	20-25 m

Ueli Kestenholz
Events: Alpine, Boardercross
Team: Scott USA
Nationality: Swiss
Snowboarding/Pro since: 89/95
Sporting Successes:
   9th place Giant Slalom ISF World Championships 1999 Val di Sole, Italy
   1st place Parallel Slalom Swiss Championships 1999
   1st place Boardercross Swatch Boarder-X World Cup 1999 Laax, Switzerland
   3rd place Giant Slalom Winter Olympics 1998, Nagano, Japan

*Ueli Kestenholz
(Photo: Alex Schelbert)*

The Freestyle Event
Half-pipe (HP)

The half-pipe competition is the crème de la crème of the snowboarding events. While in all the other events, the stopwatch is the deciding factor, in freestyle it is style that counts. The stage for this event is the half-pipe. This has been adopted from the skateboarding and BMX sports. In order to make it suitable for snowboarding, its dimensions have been adapted to suit the characteristics of the snowboard and a ramp start has been added to allow the board to pick up speed. Via a rear entry point the snowboarder rides a zigzag course through the half-pipe, gathering speed and dynamics so that he can jump up off the side-walls of the pipe.

The jumps are marked by a jury of specialists according to approved criteria. Up to 10 points are awarded for each jumping category. The criteria are: execution, degree of difficulty, height, the landing and variation. The qualifying rounds consisting of two runs decide the best eight male competitors or four in the case of ladies. The final rounds consist of the quarter-finals, semi-finals and a final.

Nicola Thost in the Half-pipe (Photo: Nitro)

Technical Data - Half-pipe (Averages)

Length:	approximately 80 - 150 m
Width:	about 15 m
Vertical Wall:	about 0.5 m
Flat Middle Section:	at least 5 m
Radius Flat to Vertical:	about 3 m

Fabien Rohrer
Events: Half-pipe
Team: Nitro Snowboards
Born: 1975
Nationality: Swiss
Sporting Successes:
 4th place Half-pipe ISF World Seeding 1999
 6th place Half-pipe ISF World Championships 1999, Val di Sole, Italy
 4th place Half-pipe Winter Olympics 1998 1998 Nagano, Japan

Nicola Thost
Events: Half-pipe, Boardercross
Team: Nitro Snowboards
Born: 1977
Nationality: German
Snowboarding/Pro since: 1990/1994
Sporting Successes:
 1st place Half-pipe ISF World Seeding 1999
 1st place Half-pipe Winter Olympics 1998 Nagano, Japan
 1st place Half-pipe Junior World Championships 1995/96
 1st place Boardercross Swatch Boarder-X Tour ,1996 Sölden, Austria.

Fabien Rohrer (Photo: Stefan Eisend)

Nicola Thost (Photo: Nitro)

Boardercross - Freeriding

If you want to get on in boardercross, you have to be a real top-class all-rounder. The race takes place on a downhill course, which is dotted with various curves, jumps and special obstacles. Up to six competitors race together at the same time.

While for other types of races it depends mainly on your riding techniques, in boardercross tactics are all important. Gaining a favourable start position, being able to react quickly to the mistakes of other competitors and being able to rapidly close any gap are the decisive factors during a race.

The various obstacles such as steep curves with or without water jumps, mogul sections and tunnels make sure that there are sufficient opportunities for the rider to show his individual strengths. The rider who has a natural feeling for the race-decisive situation is usually the one who is in the lead.

In the qualifying rounds each rider must complete two timed runs, and if he/she comes in as one of the 48 riders/24 riders he/she goes into the final rounds. In the final rounds, six competitors start off at the same time, and using the knockout system, the first three go into the next final round.

SNOW BOARD

Boardercross Final Laax 1999 (Photo: Alex Schelbert)

Technical Data - Boardercross (Averages)

Altitude Difference:	80 - 200 m
Width:	at least 30 m
Degree of difficulty:	Curves, speed, jumps, special sections

SNOWBOARD

Shaun Palmer
(Photo: Swatch)

Nillard Pilavakis
(Photo: Alex Schelbert)

Shaun Palmer
Team: Palmer Snowboards USA,
                            Swatch Pro Team
Born: 1968
Nationality: USA
Other Sports: Mountain Biking, Motocross
Snowboarding Events: Boardercross, MTB Downhill
                            and Dual-Slalom
Snowboarding/Pro since: 1982/1985
Sporting Successes:
  1st place Boardercross World Championships 1999
  Val di Sole, Italien
  1st place Boardercross Winter X-Games
  1998/99 Crested Butte, USA
  1st place Boardercross Overall Swatch Boarder-X
  1997
  2nd place MTB Downhill World Championships
  1996 Caims, Australia

Nillard Pilavakis
Team: Palmer Snowboards USA
Born: 1966
Nationality: USA
Snowboarding Events: Boardercross
Sporting Successes:
  1st place Swatch Boarder-X World Cup 1999, Laax,
  Switzerland
  4th place Boardercross World Championships 1999 Val di Sole, Italien
  2nd place Boardercross US Open 1998 Stratton Mountain, Vermont
  3rd place Boardercross Overall Swatch Boarder-X Tour 1997/98

5.2 Fun sport - Personal Styles
Freecarving - Racy Turns on the Piste

"Snowboarding" and "Carving" are two terms that are closely related with each other. Alongside the freestyle scene, with its jumps in the half-pipe and cruising in soft powdered snow, carving is the true fascination in snowboarding. Originally, the carving technique has grown out of snowboard racing. This is where absolute control in the turn and high speed form two main aims, which must come together in one. "Carving" means cutting a turn in the snow with the edge without leaving the turn line hardly at all.

This is what carving is about - turning without slipping sideways. The experienced snowboarder is able to play with centrifugal force and accelerate out of the turn, demonstrating some breathtaking banking manoeuvres in the process. To be able to execute sufficient down-pressure for real carving turns, however, it requires an active rider. It is the dream of every snowboarder to be able to make steep banking manoeuvres, as if he were on rails. With sufficient practise and a little courage, the snowboarder with ambition will no longer have to only dream of doing it all at high speed.

The carving turn is generally possible with all types of board and bindings, although it is easier to learn on boards based on the alpine style. The most important thing is to choose a suitable piece of terrain on which to practise. It is recommended that this is a flat well prepared (-essential-) slope with a lot of room. This is because there is little braking action to counter the high speeds reached in carving turns.

SNOWBOARD

Freecarving - pure (Rider: Yuji Dan / Photo: Wojciech)

Freecarving until lift-off (Rider: Chris Settele / Photo: Wojciech)

The most important point when trying out this new technique is the swing start into the turn. Contrary to the turns you have already learned about, this one starts before you get onto the fall line.

The whole of your body is directed forward and downhill. Edging occurs almost automatically. You also try to find the "right" banking into the turn by adjusting your centre of balance and the edging.

Steering also occurs almost automatically, dependant on how you tense your body according to the width of the board's sidecut, and bank into the turn. The idea is to let the board run on its edge.

Letting the board run on its edge, however, demands a good sense and feeling for your movement as well as a lot of practise. The fact that a swing turn has been successful or not can be seen in the precision of the marking that the edge carves in the snow.

For a start it is easier to concentrate only on a single turn and steer this to its ultimate end. Once you have overcome the initial fears about banking into the turn, and begin to get consistently successful, then you can begin to execute follow-on turns. The main thing with all this is to enjoy this new sense of movement. The perfect technique can be sacrificed for the simple joy of riding along and using your own personal style.

It's up to you whether you ride into the turn with a more upright stance, or whether you employ more or less upper body rotation. Also there is no specific ideal regarding the radius of the turn. Some prefer rather faster slalom turns, with constant change of direction and less banking movements, while some prefer long wide turns in which the upper body almost scrapes along the snow. The possibilities to develop and improve one's own personal riding style are almost inexhaustible.

Freeriding - Cross-country Snowboarding

"Freeriding" means riding in open terrain - off-piste. In recent times, industry and the media have portrayed the term "freeriding" as a commercial trend, but this is actually totally opposed to the real meaning for this sport. The genuine freerider associates himself with the ability to enjoy nature and freedom - the "commercial" version sees only the question of stepping over the bounds of the accepted limits of the piste without any consideration for the damage caused to nature and wildlife.

This trend is alarming on account of the great damage to the environment. It overshadows one area of snowboarding, which, when fully understood, would open up a new experience of nature and create much more fun for the normal snowboarder.

Freeriding - riding off with nature (Photo: René Marks)

The history of freeriding is as old as snowboarding itself. As the first pioneers were trying out their daring home-built boards, there was no other alternative, because of the ban on lifts in the birthplace USA, but to go off into the deep snow areas away from the ski pistes (see 'The History of Snowboarding' on Page 13). Freeriding - a combination of climbing (hiking) and downhill (snowboarding) - has deep roots, right back to the beginning of the board.

Man and Nature

The real fascination about freeriding is the link between nature, man and sport. Besides experiencing nature, with its immense beauty, one must also recognise the laws of nature and the dangers accompanying it. From this dilemma stem several interesting aspects concerning how man relates to the environment. A realistic outlook, strength of character and an awareness for his environment are the basic requirements for safely dealing with nature.

A freeride tour brings quite a new field of experience from a sporting point of view. As well as climbing up the slope, which calls for skill and stamina, the downhill phase off-piste demands new sporting qualities. If the snowboarder chooses to ride downhill on the pistes constructed for him, when he comes to riding in the mountains he will be influenced considerably by the various forms of terrain he meets.

He has to adapt his movements quickly to the constantly changing, often unknown, terrain. He must think ahead of the possible dangers and adapt each manoeuvre he executes flowingly. So that the interaction between man and nature functions properly, the following rules should always be uppermost in the mind.

Nature and the environment has uppermost priority over any freeriding activity. A high sense of safety protects man from the superiority of nature. Realistic judgement of one's own abilities protects one from physical injuries. A sense of responsibility for oneself as well as the group will lessen any risk.

SNOWBOARD

98

Climbing with nature all around (Photo: René Marks)

Planning a Freeride Tour

If you are thinking of having fun doing a freeride tour, you should first of all put a "team" together. On this type of nature "walk" there's no room for loners. Freeriding should be carried out in a group of at least two people. Unlike the regular visit to the piste there is no entry fee for a trip into nature. For this reason any tour, whether for just a day or several, must be thoroughly and professionally planned and include a high regard for the safety measures involved.

If you don't have any alpine experience, you should, in any case, engage a ski or mountain guide to lead. In some ski resorts there are organised freeride tours that include a guide and loan equipment. If you aren't sure whether freeriding is the thing for you, you should use this economical type of introduction to it.

On the other hand if you are sure you want to, and prefer to do your own plan, then, once you have chosen the area to do it in, start working together with a local ski or mountain guide. You can gather experience from him on your first tour, which you can then use to plan and carry out your own group tour later on. Using suitable maps you can plan a route that takes account of the environment and nature as well as safety, and lays down the exact scheduled timings. Exact information about weather, snow and avalanche reports are moulded provisionally into the planning - these have to be brought up-to-date directly prior to the beginning of the tour. When you all meet up for the tour, you can discuss the latest information with the guide before you set off.

Special Equipment

Freeriding equipment deserves a closer look. The normal equipment for snowboarding is already of a high technical grade. Because of safety requirements, the freerider's equipment must be even a higher standard. Equipment requirements for safety and climbing aids swell the amount of equipment needed. The length and difficulty of each tour mainly determines the amount and quality.

There should be no compromises where it concerns safety. The freerider's basic load consists of equipment to search for persons buried alive in the snow, avalanche equipment (shovel and detector) as well as a first-aid kit. All operators of the equipment must be competent and regularly trained in its use. There are several possibilities to aid climbing. The freerider can choose between snow shoes, short ski systems and separable touring boards. Additionally these can be sensibly complemented by having 'steigfelle' (ski overlays), crampons and telescopic ski sticks. The touring board is the only snowboard variant that is available as a mobile equipment to assist the rider when climbing or going downhill. When wearing short skis or snow shoes, the snowboard has to be carried on the rucksack.

The touring snowboard is constructed so that it splits down the middle. By releasing and twisting the bindings in the forward direction, the snowboarder can quickly make two short skis out of the two halves for climbing. Once the top is reached, the two halves can be put together again and give the freerider an almost perfect snowboarding feeling as he goes downhill. Manufacturers are leaning towards using the more friendly step-in systems (see Page 32 onwards) as bindings for touring snowboards, also usable with snow shoes and short skis. Just what constitutes the right climbing aid in the end, is governed by the main features of the tour planned. The deciding factors are the type of terrain, the length of the tour and any savings possible in the weight of equipment to be carried.

SNOW BOARD

101

Freeriding equipment (Rider: Shin Campos / Photo: Ken Hermer)

SNOWBOARD

Short skis with 'steigfelle' overlays and step-in bindings (Photo: K2)

The separable touring snowboard (Sketch: Nitro)

Another important item for climbing is the right clothing. To all extent and purposes, it is the same as used for normal snowboarding. However, because of the difficult conditions in the open, a good quality should be used. Here a note should be made of warmth, imperviousness and material toughness in particular. To be able to balance the thermal differences between climbing and downhill riding, the clothing should be worn in several layers, with particular attention paid to the underwear because of sweating on the climb.

In mountainous areas, of course, gloves, headwear, snow goggles and sunglasses as well as sun-protective creams are important. Round off the equipment list by having a good touring rucksack that is fitted with fastening grips for carrying the snowboard.

SNOW BOARD

Tips and Tricks:
- The weight of your equipment plays an important role.
- Changes of clothing for the different requirements of climbing and then going downhill have to be carried with you.
- Beginners or occasional riders should always think first about using hired equipment since the cost of investment in a complete set of equipment is quite high.

Suggestions for Environmental-friendly Snowboarding
- Think about how you will travel to the benefit of the environment - by bus, train?
- Use the ski-buses in the ski resort. If you have to go by car, think about car sharing.
- Follow the notices and boundary markers, which indicate obstructions, danger of avalanches and other environment notices.
- In order to avoid damage to vegetation, don't ride if the snow is not deep enough.
- Give a wide berth to sapling plots so that they stay undamaged. Avoid wildlife and rare bird reservations and fodder areas.
- For your own safety, tours, which are planned off-piste, should be lead by an expert guide who knows the dangers of avalanche in the region and local conservation circumstances.
- Obey the rule that rubbish must not be disposed of on pistes and in touring areas.

Turning nature on its head...(Rider: M. Weinländer/Photo: A. Kaiser)

Freestyle - Tricks and Jumps

If you really want to experience what is meant by living it up "snowboarding-style", you should drop in and watch the freestylers. They get together at funparks in the ski resorts, where they go about their great love all together without even getting to know each other. Their boards are like the holy grail, their clothing belongs to a cult and only those snowboarders who can do the tricks themselves understand their language. However, they all are not stereotyped - their style is "free".

And where there are no guidelines, only limited, systematic, step by step attempts at doing freestyle will help. As soon as the snowboarder has gained a certain degree of balance and feeling for the movements by doing simple exercises on the piste, he can try out his first attempts at jumping and tricks on the piste or at the funpark. Whether he tries out the well-known standard jumps with variations, or has a go at creating his own, is all a question of personal style.

Riding in the half-pipe is a further advanced form of freestyling.

Perfect Freestyling - the 360° Flip (Photos: Raichle)

After a settling-in period on the flat section of the pipe, the snowboarder can start having a go at riding up and down the steep walls. Only when he can control these manoeuvres, should he attempt jumping and landing.

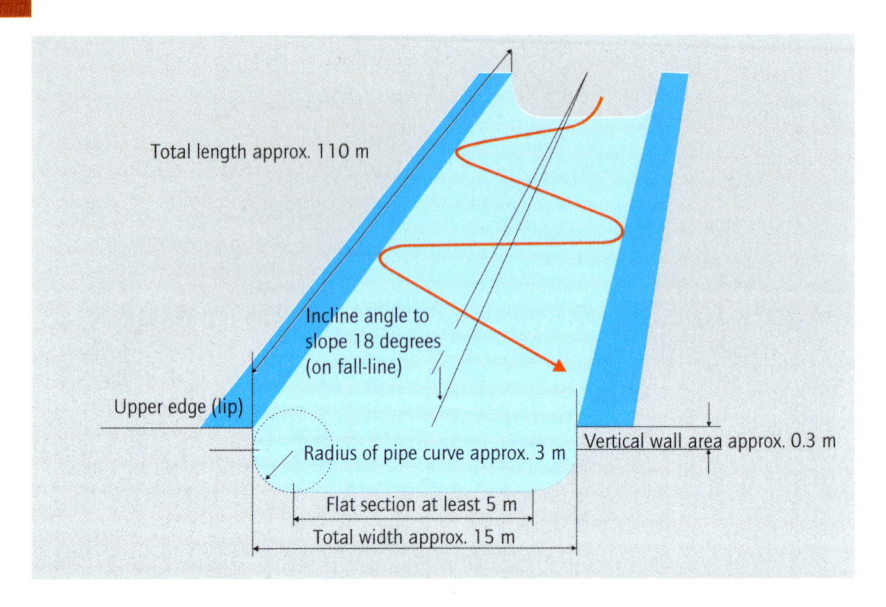

Details of the Half-pipe (Sketch: René Marks)

To be able to recognise the different jumps and tricks, the snowboarder has to learn the ABC's of jumping. The figures used are based mainly on basic jumps that are combined with one another or made more complicated. All of the jumps can be executed frontside or backside. Fakie (backwards) variations are also possible. The most common tricks are jumps (airs and aerials) with various hand positions on the board (grabs), or rotations - horizontally (spins) as well as verticals (flips). Special jumps and combinations usually bear the name of the inventor or come from the skateboard or BMX sport (one-footed air, McTwist, palm air, corkscrew).

Overview of the Basic Terminology
"Side" describes the position of the edge of the board at the start of the jump. "Frontside"- and "Backside"-jumps.
"Fakie" describes the direction of the board relative to the jump-off edge.
"Grab" describes the various positions where the rider holds the board - on the nose or the tail, between the bindings.

SNOW BOARD

"Bone" describes the way the legs are held during the jump - leg stretched out while the other is angled.
"Nosebone" front leg stretched out, rear leg angled.
"Spins" & "Flips" describes the turns about the different axes of the body. They are divided into horizontal "spins" with certain degrees (180°, 360°, 540°, 720° etc.) and "flips" in the vertical plane.

(Photo: René Marks)

Exercises on Normal Pistes
"Nose" and "Tail" -wheelies

The nose touches the snow when doing a nose-wheelie, and similarly the tail touches the snow on a tail-wheelie. These are good exercises for working up to the "nose-roll" 180° and can be done first of all in a static position by moving your weight right forward or to the rear.

Snowboarding upside-down (Photo: René Marks)

"Fakie"

Riding fakie is another name for riding backwards. It is a basic requirement for many of the freestyle jumps and riding in the half-pipe. All jumps with a 180° or 540° spin start and finish with a landing in the fakie position. The simplest way to learn riding backwards is to over-emphasise a backside turn until you are standing in the wrong direction. The weight is then placed on the "new" forward leg and you proceed in the fakie position.

A more advanced type of fakie riding, which makes the next tricks more safe, is to drift turn into the fakie position. Fakie turns should be well practised before attempting the jumping ramps. You need to be in control of your speed before making a jump in the fakie position.

"Nose-roll" 180°

The nose-roll is a half-turn about the axis of the tip of the board whilst moving forward. It is also possible to do a variation of this in the fakie position. Because the tail of the board is automatically lifted completely off the snow as the weight is placed heavily on the forward leg, this move requires a lot of pluck.

To practise this 'basic' trick, first you ride down the fall-line on a flat piece of ground. The weight is now placed heavily on the forward leg and by doing a backside rotation, the board is brought into a turning movement. After reaching the fakie position, the weight is placed back onto both legs and movement carries on in a rearwards direction.

"Ollie"

The "ollie" is the first jump variation for the freestyler. To practise this jump you do not need a jumping ramp. Instead you can do it by using your impetus. The best way is to practise it on a flat piste with some slight bumps in it. The jump is started by consciously moving the weight to the rear and at the same time bringing the front leg up. The actual jump is done by pressing heavily down and executing a sudden stretching of the rear leg upwards. The legs are tucked up under the body while you are in the air so that there is a distinct period of time in the air. Just before landing, the legs are stretched back down a little in order to absorb the shock as you set back down on the snow.

"Frontside-to-Frontside"

The frontside-to-frontside is the first trick you learn that combines two of the elements already described. This is what makes it a jump without the ramp, like the ollie. The run-up to the frontside-to-frontside is done in the fakie position. While you are in the jump, the board is brought round to face the normal forwards direction by doing a 180º twist. A similar variation is the "ollie" 180º, where, after starting off in the normal forward movement, the board is brought round by a half turn into the fakie position during the jump phase.

Practising on Piste Jumping Ramps or in Funparks

If you have practised sufficient tricks on the flat piste, and reached a certain degree of confidence and safety, you can go on and also try out new and more complicated tricks and jumps on the smaller piste jumping ramps. So that you can judge your first jumping attempts correctly, have a close look at the take-off and landing points before you try them out. So that you can judge all this well, you will find it useful to watch other jumpers on the same ground. Before each jump make sure you know which trick you want to do and try to imagine what all the necessary movements are that you will have to make, and go through them in your mind several times. For your own safety, besides this, and before you attempt any complicated combinations, you should thoroughly practise the different elements of the movement until you are able to do them perfectly.

The Basic Jump or Standard Jump

Every jump is made up of four phases. These are the start, the take-off, the aerial phase and the landing. The aerial phase is made up of a style final phase and phase where you are preparing to land. The style phase is the most important part for the freestyler. It is during this particular phase that the actual trick takes place, and the phase that 'makes' the trick in the jumper's personal 'style'. The more confidence and skill that the snowboarder shows in his jumping techniques, the more marked and varied the jumper's creativity will be in the aerial style phase. Nevertheless, don't try any wild trick ideas out when doing your first jumps over a ramp. For the basic jump, the main emphasis is in carrying out a safe take-off and landing. Initially, to ensure your own safety, the aerial style phase has to be forgotten for the time being.

Fabien Rohrer doing an "Indy Nosebone" (Photo: Nils)

The Basic Jump with "Grabs"

The basic jump with a grab is the first jump we meet that has a true aerial style phase. 'Grab' means that during the aerial, the jumper holds onto one of the steel edges of the board. For each of the various ways that the board can be held in the hand, there are different names. This depends on which side the board is 'grabbed' and with which hand.

SNOW BOARD

112

Grabbing the tail of the board - "Tail Grab" (Photo: Nitro)

The Basic Jump with "Grabs" and "Bones"

The basic jump with grabs and bones is a variation of the last jump. In addition to using a grab variation, the boarder tries to stretch out a leg while also trying to pull up the other one under the board. Here there are all sorts of variations possible with different combinations.

The Basic Jump with a "Spin"

The basic jump with a spin is a variation of jumping with a twist of the body right through the longitudinal axis. With this, the body turns in the air like a gyro. When taking-off for a 'spin', the twist is brought in just before take-off is actually achieved. It is also important that the rotation is completed before the landing so that the board doesn't end up in the snow across the direction of movement. A stage further is where all the spinning tricks are executed together with different 'grab' holds.

SNOW BOARD

114

...Summer dreams for the snowboarder (Photo: René Marks)

OVER THE EDGE AND BEYOND...

6.1 The Snowboarder's Summer Season

Of course there a lot of things that the snowboarder can busy himself with in summer while waiting for the next winter season. There are plenty of related, similar sports around such as windsurfing, surfing or in-line skating, but the real snowboarding feel is not in these. The freestyler has more chances as they can carry on quietly practising their manoeuvres skateboarding in the half-pipe or on the skateboarding parks, waiting for the next winter to come. The picture for the other types of snowboarders doesn't look so rosy. Occasionally a trip to a sandboarding hill is alright enough, but, up to now, a real solution hasn't been found.

This could all suddenly change with the advent of wakeboarding. A network of water-ski cable-ways covering the water area, and with a simple method of getting on the water, makes "snowboarding on water" a real hit for the untiring snowboarder in summer. It's certainly worth a try!

Wakeboarding

As the frustration of the season coming to an end begins to slowly spread amongst the snowboarders, in many places in Europe the water-ski cable-ways are opening their doors. The magic word is "wakeboarding". A few goes at 'snowboarding on water' should soon make the winter sportsman forget the 'vacuum' he is normally faced with in summer.

The equipment and movements are very similar to snowboarding - so there's no barrier to prevent a quick start at it. The newcomer can hire the basic equipment required for his first attempts. This consists of a wakeboard, neoprene suit and life jacket. The most usual wakeboard - a "twin-tail wakeboard" - is symmetrical, about 1.4 metres long and about 40 cm wide. The rider stands on it in bindings like on the water-ski board and the stance is the same as a freestyler uses. To improve the stability of the board in the water, it is fitted with a fin at the front and the rear. Because of its symmetrical shape, the board can be used in both directions and permits numerous possibilities for tricks by virtue of this.

SNOW BOARD

Wakeboarding - the new sporting trend (Photo: René Marks)

Movements are the same as snowboarding (Photo: René Marks)

SNOW BOARD

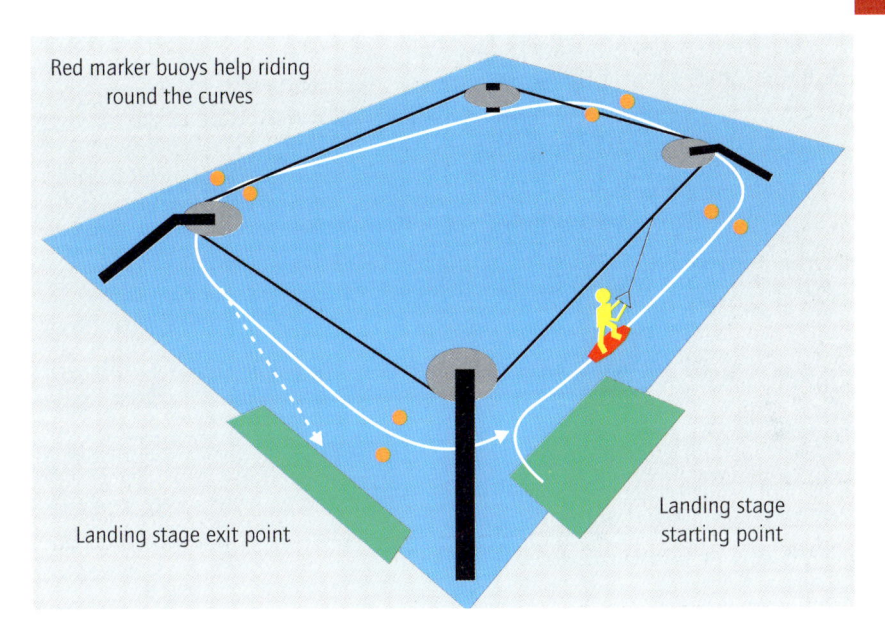

The details of a water ski cable-way (Sketch: René Marks)

The wakeboarder uses a landing stage to take-off from and is hooked into a cable-way, which runs round a fixed course and pulls him round on the lake (see the sketch above). At the end of the course he can either let go of the line as he nears the start point or go round again. The cable-way speed for wakeboarding is between 30 kmh and a maximum of 38 kmh.

For most snowboarders the switch to this is relatively easy. Only the take-off and steering the wakeboard need a little getting used to. The newcomer must watch out, particularly when the line, hooked into the cable-way travelling at a steady speed as it does, comes under tension at the start. By leaning backwards and with slightly bent arms, the boarder can counteract the jerking movement and avoid the tip of the board dipping under the surface of the water. After 1-2 hours, the initial difficulties are mostly forgotten and the first few clear rounds have been accomplished.

In Germany, there are about 40 water-ski cable-ways, which sufficiently satisfy the desires of the wakeboarder fun-seekers. In the meanwhile there are about 10,000 active participants under the spell of this sport with 75 organised water-ski and wakeboard-clubs in which to carry it out.

If you have an ambition to become a "waker", this new sport offers a lot of chances for fun and competitive sporting at national and world championship levels. The cable-way competitions are a kind of 'freestyle contest'. Run in two rounds, the boarder can demonstrate a random number of manoeuvres and jumps, which are marked against three criteria - technical difficulty, height and creativity.

Sandboarding

A further alternative open to the snowboarder in summer is "sandboarding". Besides the sand pistes in California, Australia and South Africa, 'Monte Kaolino', near Nuremberg, Germany is the centre of sandboarding in Europe. As early as 1985 the first 'pioneers' began riding down the sand masses. Snowboarding legends such as Peter BAUER and Petra MÜSSIG have even ventured to experience boarding of a different kind at Monte Kaolino. The hill is 110 m high and consists of over 30 million tons of quartz sand and provides top sandboarding pleasure. You get sufficient momentum on steep downhill piste slopes to overcome the sand's resistance.

SNOW BOARD

Parallel Slalom at the Sandboard World Championship 1999 (Photo: T. Hönig)

The Mecca for Sandboarders in Germany - "Monte Kaolino" (Photo: T. Hönig)

Last year's latest board is the top choice for this 'sand-papering' pleasure on the quartz surface. When it comes to tuning your board there are no limits to the boarder's ingenuity and fantasy. The tuning freak's repertoire ranges from masking the edges to treating the underside with Vaseline and washing-up liquid.

The availability of a lift, beginners' courses and on-the-spot gastronomy all make a visit to this sandboard location a complete alternative for fun for the insatiable snowboarder.

Once a year sees Monte Kaolino receiving the world's best sandboarders turning up for the Sandboarding World Championship. In addition to a full programme of music, parties and shows, you will see the best sandboarders in the world competing in slalom, boardercross and high-speed events.

6.2 Snowboarding Camps - Snow & Fun

A relaxed atmosphere, nice and easy-going people and snowboarding; every now and then they like to have a little party. If you simply can't get enough then you should take part in a snowboarding camp. There are several fortnightly camps in Germany, Austria and Switzerland that are organised by professional tour groups. These are aimed at all groups from the beginner to the half-pipe specialist. There is also an increase in the camps, which specialise in looking after the rider who has ambitions. These are supervised by well-known snowboarding professionals. The camps also often have skateboarding on the programme.

It is also now a common thing that you can find resort camps in Scandinavia, the USA and Canada, for example. Many are based in different star-rated hotels and the organisers take trouble to ensure that the all-round service available is as perfect as possible.

Snowboarding - a different view (Photo: René Marks)

Besides the normal service offered by hotels, the snowboarders are offered special programmes with video games, snowboarding video evenings and parties with "special DJs" to get them in the right mood. The snowboarders are also taken well care of on the piste, where there is a range of things from funparks, coverage of riding techniques and analysis by video, to demonstrations of the latest equipment by the manufacturers on tap. Kitted out with the latest equipment, everyone then goes off onto the piste.

Snowboarding guides take the participants off through the skiing areas and give the various groups, each at different levels of skill, tips and show them tricks. Often the rider who has ambition will find courses of instruction available on the half-pipe or slalom runs. The remainder is all up to improvisation - a little mogul for a cool jump; a little hop to a little tune on the walkman or a lunch with friends in the next ski hut - everyone can experience a lot of fun at these camps. They are well worth a try.

One of the larger summer camps in Europe is the SPC 55 Skate & Snow Camp in Mayrhofen in Austria. Here, from the middle of May to the middle of August, you can find combined snow and skateboarding weekly courses running, which offer a full programme with lots of attractions. All-inclusive are half-board accommodation, the lift pass and free entry to the King Size Super Park as well as to the indoor skating park. During the special theme weeks, such as the "Starfish week" or the "Mute week", the customers, mostly 16-22 year old freestylers, can choose from a large palette of activities.

Snowboarding magazines, party specials and the top teams from the big snowboarding firms offer these youths non-stop action. The SPC board fan can pick something to do with snow or skating or a fun activity from the programme running from 9 o'clock in the morning to late into the night. In the fun section, those seeking mental preparation for the piste can choose from a large selection of computer games and videos. On the large-screen television he can not only see the professionals and their riding style, but also his own from the daily video analysis shoots. This is all rounded off by surfing on the Internet using the computers in the hotel's game zone.

The week's party calendar is also worth taking note of. On Monday the week begins with a 'Welcome' dinner. From Tuesday onwards there's one party after the other; beach party, bonfire party, and three evenings in the hotel's own 'Arena Disco' with special DJs and 'live gigs' getting all the board fans into the party mood. With the grooving still ringing in his ears, next morning the snowboarder can relax a little more quietly in the "Chill Zone" in the King Size Super Park. This is when the SPC freestylers get down to the real work of the day.

Choice in the 'members only' King Size Super Park is overwhelming. Besides two 150-metre long half-pipes there are snowboarding fun-boxes, gaps and rails available. At the bottom there is a lift for the stressed-out freestyler, which saves him sweating his way back up to the top.

To assist the beginner groups there are trained freestyle instructors and professional instructors for the speciality courses. Even a session of private training with a top rider is normally not a problem.

Professionals show the way...(Rider: Pekka Vali/Photo: Richard Walch)

During the whole of the summer, the professionals train in the SPC camp - a good opportunity to get some new ideas for one's jumps. The slightly smaller "Indoor Skate Park" is almost as well equipped as the King Size Super Park, and here is where you will find comparatively good mini-ramps, fun-boxes and rails that can give the snowboarder a change from being on the piste.

Slightly smaller are also the participants on the "Junior Weeks". With parental permission and with the organiser's concept of full-time supervision, the 8-15 year old up-and-coming freestylers can try out all the aspects of the full SPC programme - except the parties. This is the future concept for the insatiable snowboarding youth - real KING SIZE!

6.3 Virtual Snowboarding
Internet & Co

Snowboarding was always one of those kind of sports that had not only fascinated fans on the piste. The board fan's interest in developing a particular *joie de vivre* by snowboarding was always present. To meet up at parties or in the shop, to exchange ideas about the latest tricks and to chat about boarding trends, music and the rag trade was always one of their trademarks.

Since the time that the computer has become routine in everyday life, a great deal has been done for the snowboarder in this branch. The Internet allows us to have almost unlimited communication access to boarders all over the world. On the homepages belonging to manufacturers, snowboarding magazines and winter sport regions you can find every possible piece of information about the subject of snowboarding.

SNOWBOARD

125

F2 Snowboarding news on the Internet

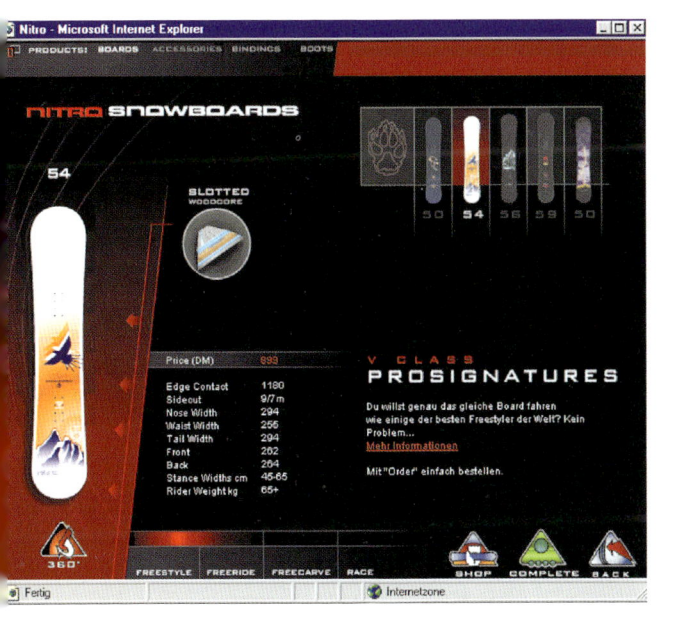

Nitro product's website on the Internet

When buying equipment or planning a holiday you can find the latest tips on it about products, consumer tests and holiday offers. You can pose any outstanding questions you have very quickly to the companies by using e-mail. If the personal touch when surfing on the Internet is needed, then you can go straight into the special 'chat-rooms' where you can exchange information and have a 'chat' about the latest news and trends with snowboarding colleagues all over.

The ease and speed of obtaining information this way gives the snowboarder fresh methods of communication, which, with the expanding volume of the Internet, will continue to improve to the consumer's benefit. In a section at the end of this book is a selection of Internet web addresses. For those who prefer to look for themselves, the various search engines can be used by inputting the keyword to find the world-wide snowboard homepages.

Computer Games

If you have ever looked around the computer games department of the large electronic market houses, you will know that this kind of recreational activity doesn't only have a magical attraction for children and youths. Sophisticated sports simulation, such as snowboarding, has been brought onto a very high technical level by the development of the PC computer hardware and special game consoles.

Snowboard games are available for the three main games platforms - PC, Sony Playstation and Nintendo 64. Operation is controlled over a menu programme and very easily understood by computer beginners as well as all youths.

In 1997, "Coolboarder" (Sony Playstation) came on to the market as the first snowboarding game. This classic is now available in Version 3 and its play options have been widely expanded. As with the Nintendo 64 game, "180º Snowboarding", the boarder can play all the options, from half-pipe to boardercross competitions. Different boards, numerous trick possibilities and downhill courses add the finishing touches to give a genuine feeling for the piste. If you want to imagine stepping into the shoes of top riders such as Daniel FRANCK or Terje HAAKONSEN, you could

SNOW BOARD

127

The snowboarding feeling - the computer game "Xgames (Graphics:ESPN/Electronic Arts)

Virtual "Grinding" in the "Xgames Proboarder" (Graphics:ESPN/Electronic Arts)

choose no better a game than the PC game "X Games Proboarder". To the tones of music such as "Foo Fighters" you can emulate the world elite's riding style.

Feel like an interactive game? Grab the game pad and let's dip into the world of snowboard games. With the CD loaded, we start on the ramp to have a go at a boardercross race, individually or in competition with other rider players. After you have chosen rider characteristics, type of board and race course profile, you press the button and start the game. By pressing another button on the game pad you can increase the speed of your rider, and by gently nudging the direction control, you can keep him safely on track.

After you have negotiated several steep curves, you have to decide whether you go through the woods or leap off an enormously high ramp. The jump over the ramp is not quite so successful - the combination of buttons selected have unfortunately caused it to be too flat. But the landing has been cleverly corrected and you've got the board going in the right direction again..... Computer games can be quite exciting.

Videos

You can get even nearer to the action with one of the numerous videos about snowboarding. The selection on offer is very large - from instructional videos to ones about riding techniques and on to videos on tricks for the half-pipe fan.

The section on riding techniques is particularly interesting for the beginner and occasional boarder. Using video sequences, the beginner learns each step systematically along the way. Snowboard instructors demonstrate the different movements and exercises exactly and tips are given about the possible difficulties and causes of mistakes.

A visit to the snowboarding school cannot be replaced by these videos, but they are extremely suitable for preparation to go to one, and for 'revising'. Videos of one's own riding can also help the snowboarder to improve his style. Besides the fun of seeing oneself on video during the evening viewing to check yourself out. Crass mistakes can be quickly noted and corrected the next morning.

Half-pipe and trick action videos are also very popular with snowboarders. Inspired by the BMX and skateboarding world, most of them have music accompaniments and show all the possible and impossible tricks done by top riders and snowboarding freaks.

Exotic filming scenes, lots of lifestyle and a few clips of unedited shots make these videos top money-spinners amongst youth and the freaks - a real top-class pleasure to the eye and the ear.

That's the route... (Photo: René Marks)

7....AND EVERYTHING ELSE THAT'S IMPORTANT!
7.1 The Ideal Snowboarding Regions

The first white flakes, signalling the coming winter, are dancing outside the window. The observer is fascinated by the white brilliance, which is slowly covering the tarmac and he feels an itch starting in his feet. He begins to imagine how it will feel when he gets his beloved snowboard up from the cellar and when he will be able to go off - where else but up into the mountains. But exactly where should he go?

If you have been going to the same snowboarding resort for years, you will have few problems as you will know what's in store for you. The inquisitive and those who love to experiment and want to go off to learn about a new region will have a little more difficulty. Not every one of the numerous winter sports resorts is necessarily suitable for snowboarding. Many of the well-established winter sports resorts are more suitable for skiing and offer very few possibilities for the snowboarder to put himself through the paces he desires. There are, however, several factors to be taken into account when looking for a suitable region, and these will be well worth following to ensure you find a crowning example.

The most important factors in the ideal snowboarding resort are to have an optimal piste and availability of snow lifts. While the skier is looking for a challenge with numerous steeper sections in the piste and lots of moguls, the snowboarder can get the best out of his sport on the flatter and wider slopes. Thus a winter sports area with mainly easy to medium difficulty pistes will be the best one for the snowboarder specialist.

But how will the deep snow experts and freestyle freaks get on? Some resorts, where there is sufficient snow, have considerable potential with safe and easily accessible freeride slopes alongside the prepared pistes.

SNOWBOARD

132

(Photo: René Marks)

SNOW BOARD

Snowboarding in Laax, Switzerland (Photo: Alex Schelbert)

The glacier region Kitzsteinhorn, Austria (Photo: René Marks)

In the same way, for the freestylers amongst us, the last few years has shown a change towards the positive. Where, earlier, many pistes and lifts were barred for snowboarders, often nowadays it's quite the opposite.

On some sections of the piste, proper freestyle funparks with numerous different types of terrain and lots of jumping possibilities have sprung up, where practically only snowboarders can be found. Also professionally constructed half-pipes and special boardercross routes are now more commonly found in many places.

Besides having ideal slopes to go down and sufficient freestyle possibilities, of course having suitable aids to climb up the slopes is absolutely essential in order to experience a successful snowboarding outing. With no other alternative available, if you have experienced and put up with mile-long lifts on a snowboard, you will know that lifts like these are much more exhausting than snowboarding itself.

Therefore, when selecting a resort, it's recommended that you chose one with an adequate number of chair lifts or cabin lifts. You will then be able to take a rest on the way up, so that your strength will carry you through to the end of a day's snowboarding.

For the snowboarder who wants to carry on learning, then the availability of a selection of snowboarding schools is also an important factor. To this end you can go almost anywhere of choice without any worries, because nowadays there are snowboarding schools in all the winter sports areas.

However, for lots of snowboarders on holiday, it's not just only a question of having super snowboarding every day, but also the possibility of enjoying that special snowboarding joie de vivre every night. Besides noting the points above, the corresponding availability on the après ski scene in the diverse boarder establishments should also be taken into account.

Now that you know which criteria are important in choosing the ideal snowboard resort, the question is where do you get the corresponding information?

SNOWBOARD

To get a general overview of the ski regions in the Alps from a reliable source, it is recommended to have a look in one of the current ski atlases. Here you will find sufficient information about all the factors we have mentioned already. Besides this, they usually include an evaluation of the skiing areas against particular different categories. The categories give clear recommendations about which area is best for which group. You will also find information (under the keyword 'snowboarding scene') about which winter sports areas have the right environment for snowboarders.

A ski atlas will also have additional information about current prices for ski passes and accommodation. Since in many ski regions, particularly where snowboarding takes place, there are lots of new things appearing, and one can expect that prices shown do not remain static over the years, you should try to get information from an as up-to-date as possible ski atlas. In this connection it is worth finding a ski guide on the internet. You will find some useful web addresses in the section about internet addresses (see Page 163).

If you require more specialised information and the latest news from the winter sports regions of the Alps you should treat yourself and have a look at a snowboarding magazine. For example you will find regular reports by professional snowboarders about suitable downhill runs for freeriders in their favourite resorts.

Besides this you will also find real insider tips about reasonably priced food and accommodation, and where the best parties are taking place.

Well-equipped with all this information you will surely be able to enjoy some good experiences on your next holiday.

7.2 Snowboarding Courses - Up onto the Board

Snowboarding should be fun. When snowboarding, many just want to experience a sense of a different and free life, and be able to develop their own style, unshackled by rigid rules. To be more precise, the main thing is to be able to start snowboarding easily and freely. In preparing for the countdown to 'S' (for snowboarding) Day, magazines and beginner's books will help the newcomer to get over the first psychological hurdles. The snowboarder of the future will get his equipment - loaned from a good friend, who will give tips gained from his own experiences of his first riding attempts.

It will soon become clear during the somewhat difficult beginner's exercises, that the friend may well be a good rider but much less a good instructor. As a result you should carefully consider the choice between your 'private' instructor and the route to a snowboard school.

The snowboarding course - ready for the first lesson (Photo: Achim Schmidt)

The fact that a course at a snowboarding school doesn't necessarily mean that rigid teaching methods are used is borne out by the individually formed teaching methods encouraged by snowboarding associations. If you choose carefully, then an introductory course at a reliable snowboarding school is the sure way to quickly get into having the fun one hoped for at the beginning.

The Right School for Snowboarding

If you have decided on attending a snowboarding course, you will have to find a suitable one. When researching the local schools you should check for qualifications and snowboarding Association certificates of competence. In Germany, for example, there are schools recognised by the Deutschen Skilehrerverband (DSLV, German Ski Instructors Association). They guarantee the participant first-class training by qualified personnel and ensure that there is an optimum programme for the course. In most cases, when you begin a course, you will require all the equipment. This you may be able to borrow or, as in some instances, you may simply have to buy. In this case it is worth considering choosing a school with an adjacent shop and hire outlet. Advice for the beginner will be on hand here and questions answered about equipment and the choice of course. Besides a choice of taking part in a group course or individual training, the selection of courses will normally range from half-day introductory courses to a complete 5-day session. A good snowboarding school will have advanced courses for riding techniques and special training sessions for the advanced in the areas of carving, slalom and freestyle tricks on offer to round off their programme.

Tips and Tricks:
- You should be able to buy or hire boards.
- You should be able to hire or test a range of different boards.

The Course Programme

The introductory and one-day courses are for you to get a short introduction and orientation into the sport of snowboarding. The winter sportsman, still undecided which way to go, and the crossover skier can gain a quick insight on how to snowboard doing these courses. If, after this, he gets a real snowboarding fever, he should then undertake one of the 3- or 5-day courses. With a daily rate of three to five hours from a qualified instructor, the snowboarder will get a systematic introduction into the basic techniques of snowboarding.

The content of the course is designed along training concepts specially developed for snowboarding and conventional training methods from skiing. On your first shaky steps you will find exercises using your teacher or another pupil as a partner to help. This is because, at the start, a strong sense of balance and feeling for the movements are very much in demand. In the same way, initially your stamina will be stretched, particularly on the first day of your introduction to snowboarding.

A well known aid for practising the gliding and canting movements is the carousel. This is a revolving cross apparatus where up to two or three pupils hold onto the bars of the cross. Dependent on the direction the cross is turned in, the pupils can practise backside and frontside exercises as it turns. The much used methods of "follow the leader" and "taking direction from behind" - as used in skiing - can also be used on the snowboard course for some riding exercises. In order to put the exercises into practice on the piste, the instructions for the exercises are called out by the instructor, or can be practised by instructions to negotiate obstacles such as cones, poles or gloves placed down on the snow.

SNOWBOARD

The 3-Day Snowboard Course	Day 1	Day 1	Day 3
1. Warming up programme and stretching exercises	■	■	
2. Stance - Goofy or Regular			
3. Adjusting the Board and Bindings			
4. Carrying and Laying down the board			
5. Getting into the bindings and standing up			
6. Falling down and standing up again			
7. Turning the strapped on board			
8. Foot paddle with one foot in the binding	■		
9. The basic stance			
10. Jumping up with the board			
11. The slow glide			
12. Canting, slide-slipping and braking			
13. Riding diagonally	■		
14. Using the pull bar lift			
15. Uphill swing turn			
16. Using the chair lift and dismounting		■	■
17. Using the T-bar lift			
18. Basic drift turn front + back			
19. Basic drift turn front + back		■	
Variations			
terrain, speed, turn radius and			
negotiating poles			
20. Using all types of lift + different piste types			■
21. Downhill runs on the blue piste			
Exercising different riding techniques			
different terrain and obstacles			

An overview of the 3-Day snowboarding course (Graphics: René Marks)

With a group size of 5-8 persons, the instructor has sufficient time to give each of them assistance and individual coaching to correct faults. In small groups it is also possible to progress well with the learning and exercises, using a partner to get over any worries about unfamiliarity and make corrections quickly, help enormously. So that a relaxed and personal atmosphere exists amongst the group, it is important that the same snowboarding instructor is able to remain with the same group up until the end of the course.

Altogether, an introductory course should consist of about 15-20 individual exercises, dependent on the aim. The exercises should guarantee that the pupil, at the end, will be able to control the board safely in simple terrain. The aim will have been achieved when the pupil manages to safely execute a run down a blue piste consisting of various types of obstacle. In all this, the use of a lift, especially the pull bar one, and being able to make turns of different radii cleanly are particularly important.

Tips and Tricks:
- Each session should begin with a short warm-up and body stretching programme, because the unfamiliar movements of snowboarding put a heavy strain on the body.
- The 5-day course gives the pupil more time to absorb the lessons and allows for gradual correction of mistakes if certain things are not successful at the first attempt.
- A change in the course curriculum is feasible if the group participants are ready for such a change.

7.3 Hired Equipment

A complete set of equipment comprising of snowboard, bindings and boots -all specifically tuned for the rider - is one of the prerequisites for rapid success in learning. Freeride and freestyle boards are particularly good for the learning phase because of their user-friendly riding characteristics and simplicity in being able to turn the board.

Regarding boots and matching bindings, professional trainers prefer the hardboot and plate binding, which give the beginner a good, direct contact with the snow and a safe feeling when riding. When the somewhat stiffer feeling of the boot doesn't suit you, then a changeover to soft boots with shell bindings can be made.

One development in equipment, which is good for the beginner, is the comfortable and convenient method afforded by the modern step-in binding mechanism. More and more snowboard schools are now using this type of binding, thus saving the pupil the annoyance of having to clip-up in the snow.

Tips and Tricks:
- In order to keep apace with technical changes, hired equipment should not be older than 2-3 years.
- When collecting the equipment, it must be visually checked over to make sure it is in good condition (cracks, corners broken, mechanical defects).
- The regular use of ski boots in the long run is not recommended on grounds of safety. They are, however, sufficient for trying out things at the beginning.

7.4 Snowboarding for Children - Fun Learning

Children generally find snowboarding cool and trendy. They have watched young snowboarders on television or seen pictures in magazines where they are doing spectacular tricks in the half-pipe. They also want to be able to do all this of course. Amongst their circle of friends, they often find children of the same age who have already started snowboarding and enthusiastically tell stories about their last winter holiday and show off the photos. For all those children, who have finally managed to convince their parents that they want to learn this trendy sport of snowboarding, the fun must start right from the very word go. Snowboarding can provide a super experience for children as long as they have relatively rapid success learning, and the new sport remains cool during the introductory phase.

The right start already begins with the choice of the correct snowboarding equipment. What kind of children's clothing is best suitable for snowboarding? Which is the best snowboard to use?

The question of whether to attend a snowboarding school, and which form should be selected, must also be addressed. Knowledge about the essential points that go to make up equipment and training suitable for children helps to form the right decision, so that nothing stands in the way of making a 'cool' beginning.

Children's snowboarding - cool kids!
(Photo: Nicole Zahn-Bechen)

Snowboards for Children

There are certain points that must be particularly noted when equipping the future mini snowboarders. Children's snowboards are not just simply small versions of the grown-ups' ones. For example, a short board for a grown-up has a greater tension factor and more sidecut than a child's snowboard. Besides this, a grown-ups' foot is larger and so the board will be generally too wide. A 'real' child's snowboard has been constructed to match body proportions and developing strength. It will have the ideal length if it reaches as high as the chin, or at a maximum, to the nose.

Different sizes of children's snowboards (Photos: Nitro)

The width of the child's board is proportional to the size of the foot and the laid down angle of the binding. The ends of the bindings must not extend over the sides of the board at any point. The optimum distance between the bindings must be adjusted by a specialist in a sports shop, and the priority will be to ensure that the safety of the child is the uppermost consideration.

Many of the snowboard manufacturers now offer special boards for children. The child's board, complete with bindings, will cost between £125-£175. The growing child will generally be able to use the same board only for one or two winters by which time he will have outgrown the board.

In order to keep costs down, it is recommended that you purchase from a sports shop that also has boards for hire. There will then be a possibility that you will be able to exchange your old board when purchasing a new one. Considering that there will only be a single snowboarding holiday per winter season, hiring a board will often be the cheaper option. You should always do this on the spot in the resort so that if you aren't happy, or there are faults in the equipment, you will be able to get direct help.

Children's Boots and Bindings

It is only in the last few years that something positive has occurred in the area of special children's snowboarding boots. In the 1995/96 season, paradoxically, there was not one hardboot available on the market for children although many manufacturers were offering the matching plate bindings for them. Up until then, children could only use normal ski boots on a board with plate bindings. For health and pure functional reasons this should be avoided at all costs. The construction and function of current ski boots is not suitable for the typical movements done on a children's snowboard, and can lead to painful strains and stresses.

In the meanwhile, industry has answered the call of the children's demands and there are both soft boots and hard boots on offer for them. Because boots and bindings must be seen as a functional entity, they should be always bought together. But which binding system is best for children?

SNOW BOARD

Various examples of children's boots and bindings (Photos: Raichle, Nitro)

For little children up to seven years old as well as older child beginners, the recommendation is soft boots with clip bindings. Soft boots - as the name suggests - allow plenty of freedom of movement on the board, so that tricks can be more easily attempted. Because they are comfortable to wear and they don't weigh much at all relatively, they are extremely suitable for playing around in during pauses in snowboarding.

From an age of seven years and upwards a hardboot with a plate binding can be used. The advantage of the hardboot is that they are easy to open and do up, as well as easier when getting into and out of the bindings. Besides this the transfer of power from the hardboot directly onto the board is greater than with the soft boot. On the other hand, the harder and heavier boots limit the child's freedom of movement and are often found to be less pleasant. Hardboots should be fitted out, where possible, with a walking and standing mechanism so that there is a greater freedom of movement. Children who can already ski, and are therefore used to ski boots, will not find the change to wearing the snowboarding hardboot difficult. The decision whether to wear the alpine oriented variant has to be left up to the child itself.

Children's Clothing

Functionality must be the uppermost priority when choosing children's clothing. Functional and suitable child's clothing is now available en masse at reasonable prices. The cheapest solution is to buy next winter's clothing as the current season ends. Many shops have clearance sales and many items are on offer at up to 50% discount.

Regarding functionality for children, the same principles and criteria are valid as for grown-up snowboarders (see Chapter 3.4 Functional 'Clothes Maketh Man'). Above all, trousers and gloves should be absolutely watertight to allow for children playing around and having a lot of contact with the snow. An additional recommendation is the use of wrist, elbow and knee protectors, like skateboarding and in-line skating. You can usually find the protectors being sold cheaply as a complete set. Because of the bright glare and intensity of the sun, children should never spend a day snowboarding without a cap or woolly hat and sunglasses.

Snowboard Lessons for Children

The type and method of snowboard lessons for children differs basically from that for grown-ups. For them, the main aim is to learn the pure technical snowboarding skills, while for children, the main thing in the lesson is to learn by playing and enjoying the experience. The fun gained by this free play method, and being in the open air together with nature, is particularly important for children coming from urban areas with often limited play and games possibilities.

The ideal age for a child to start off into 'snowboarding life' is elementary school age (7-12 years old). At this age the physical prerequisites such as stamina and strength are well enough developed, so that they are capable of meeting the challenges of a full day's snowboarding instruction.

As far as motor skills and capabilities are concerned, the 10-12 year old age group is considered as the best age for learning. Children learn new skills very quickly at this age of their development (self-starters). Also their powers of concentration are well advanced enough to be able to follow longer periods of instruction.

Of course, even the younger child can get a whiff or two of snowboarding. Children aged 5-7 years old show just as much interest in their environment as their elders. They also possess a good willingness to learn. However, their attention spans are very much shorter and with this the demand for play and games greater. Physical development is not yet advanced enough to be able to really control such a large and cumbersome piece of equipment as the snowboard.

These factors concerning the younger children must be taken into consideration for their instruction. At this age, the concept of learning through playing is very important. Within this concept the idea of gliding along on different pieces of equipment such as toboggans and plastic sledge plates can be brought into use. Also the use of so-called Big Foot skis can provide an alternative aid.

Big Foot for children and grown-ups (Photos: Kneissl)

Big Foot are short skis about 50-65 cm long, which resemble over-dimensional large feet from their outward appearance. After a short familiarity phase, pretty much every child can soon walk, turn and move sideways with confidence on them. Playful experimentation also serves to train the children to keep their ideal balance. They can also learn several important characteristics about them, which can be used in snowboarding.

They are also effective as an aid to the first 'standing' gliding movements in the snow and learning to use the steel edges. With previous experience of a snow sport and gliding on the snow gained on Big Foot, changing over to the snowboard no longer creates any difficulty. Big Foot can also be used to create a relaxing break for fun in between snowboarding training periods for all groups, irrespective of ability and age.

Regardless of the age that a child starts snowboarding, the first training periods should be spent in an approved snowboarding school. Learning in a group of the same ages provides good motivation and gives the children a lot of fun together. But, as a layman, how do you know which snowboard school for children is the right one, and does it have competent child instructors?

To ensure that the learning experience can be successful and full of fun, there are a few factors that parents can take note of when choosing a snowboard school for their nippers.

Factors concerning the choice of a snowboarding school suitable for children:

- The course should last the whole of the day and not only half-days.
- The snowboarding school offers the children a complete programme inclusive of a midday meal and playtime breaks.
- The snowboarding school has lots of playthings available such as climbing bars, balls, giant play cubes, shovels etc., as well as sledge type equipment such as toboggans, large plastic bags and plastic sledge plates.
- There is a funpark on the school grounds with comical figures and differing types of conditions such as bumpy runs or a section for deep snow.
- The school has a special course programme for children. The school has a prospectus containing details of things available for the groups of different aged children.
- At the end of the course there is a final competition or a party for all the children.

If all, or at least most of these conditions are present, it is just a question of luck that you will find a 'real' child's snowboard instructor. In many respects, a children's instructor is faced with different challenges than one who teaches grown-ups. He must be able to adapt himself to the world of children and be able to speak their 'language'. Beyond that he must be able to conduct a number of different exercise variations so that the children do not get bored quickly. The success of any instruction and the ability for the children to have fun is very dependent on the commitment and creativity of the instructor.

A children's snowboarding course - training with a partner (Photo: Nicole Zahn-Bechen)

At the end of a day's snowboarding, the parents should find out from their children how it has gone, how they have enjoyed it and what they have learned. After a snowboarding course over several days, normally the children will be able to negotiate a simple piste and show off their first turns to their parents. They will be able now to look forward, thoroughly enthusiastically and excitedly, to the next winter holiday.

7.5 Snowboarding - With Safety

Thank God - it was alright in the end! The snowboard landed deep into a pile of snow right next door to the little ski-lift hut. Its owner had stuck it into the snow on the slope above and had been chatting with friends. The board fell over and shot at top speed down the hill.

So that snowboarding remains just fun and doesn't turn into almost a nightmare like in the story above, there are some important safety rules that every snowboarder should learn. Where it concerns the safety of all users on the piste, everyone must be extra careful concerning equipment, use of the piste and the environment.

Safe Snowboarding

Having good, functioning equipment is the first step towards safe snowboarding. Your own ability should be the measure in choosing the right equipment. This includes the board as well as the bindings, which should be adjusted to the individual and should come up to the very latest standards. Because of the various stresses and strains that can be experienced, use of ski boots should be avoided where possible, and the purchase of special snowboarding models considered.

You should make sure that your clothing is warm enough. Extra padding in the knee and seat of the pants give the snowboarder protection against contact

SNOW BOARD

The author's advice is...Not this way! (Photo: Frank Gille)

with snow in these areas. Good protective gloves are just as important. Beginners will find they rely on them a lot, because they will use them to stand up after falling down often.

Even the best type of board will not steer itself. It's all up to the rider - his self judgement and a good physical condition are the main points to ensure a safe run. Snowboarding shouldn't begin only on the piste. It's more a question of continually working up to the winter season. By doing stamina training and other sports, such as bicycling, in-line skating and gymnastics, you can really make yourself fit for winter. Don't forget to carry out a short warming up and stretching exercise session before you start your day's snowboarding. The first few yards on the piste will be easier if you are fit. The chances of injury will be lower and the initial starting difficulties will be quickly got over.

Following on from the rider and equipment, there is the question of the other piste users. In the throng on the piste, everyone should watch out for the others. The FIS Rules constitute the "Highway Code" for safety on the piste. Additionally, every snowboarder must take into consideration the different styles used by skiers and snowboarders in order to avoid further risks. A defensive style of riding will allow everyone the chance of arriving home safe and sound.

Tips and Tricks:

- Equipment is adjusted to the individual, is modern and in good condition.
- The board and the rider are joined together by a safety leash. When carrying the board the leash is wrapped round the wrist or used as a carrying strap.
- The board must be placed down on the snow with the binding facing down into it in order to prevent it sliding away.
- Clothing should match the prevailing weather conditions and should be suitable to meet the strains it will be placed under.
- The particularly important accessories are gloves, a hat, sunglasses and sun cream.
- The rider is in a fit condition having done special preparatory training. By carrying out daily warm-up exercises and muscle stretching exercises he will minimise the danger of injury.
- As a precaution, the beginner learns the basic actions of how to fall down and stand up safely. He should be able to do all the basic actions and movements before he uses the piste and the lifts.
- Every person who goes on the piste should know all the FIS Ski and Snowboarding Rules.
- Defensive riding, a realistic self assessment of one's ability and watching out for others on the piste are 'musts'.
- The snowboarder must take account of the different styles of both skiers and snowboarders - the radius of the turn for snowboarding is mainly a larger one.

Equipment Safety Checks

Prior to the beginning of the season, equipment should be checked over by a specialist or yourself, if you have sufficient expertise.

The Board and Bindings

- Check the board over for damage and rips, which could endanger the rider or shorten the board's life.
- Check the skiing surface and steel edges of the board for damage and get a ski specialist to prepare the board (waxing the surface and honing the steel edges).
- Test all the parts of the binding for condition and tighten up any screws with the correct tool - this also applies to the screws that hold the bindings onto the board. All the screwed parts should be treated with special safety lacquer obtained from an ironmongers before being tightened.
- Check the binding mechanisms over such as joints, clamps, buckles and moving surfaces to make sure they work freely and apply a drop of oil or special preservative spray where needed.
- Check the position and stability of the board's safety leash, both at the board and the leg fixture ends.
- The course should last the whole of the day and not only half-days.
- The anti-slip pad between the bindings should be in a good condition so that the next lift journey doesn't turn into a 'slip-up'.

The Boots

- Check the plastic shells of the hardboots over for rips and worn places, taking particular note of the points where there are clamps and buckles.
- Check the material, stitching and tie-ups of the soft boots for worn out places.
- Check any clamps, buckles and joints and make sure they are still functioning.
- On the hardboots check the anti-slip part of the plastic soles.
- Check the cleats, clamps and the pegs of the step-in bindings for wear. Test that they are functioning and check the screw mountings.

SNOW BOARD

154

Good equipment guarantees that the joy of snowboarding will not be ruined (Photo: René Marks)

The 10 FIS-Rules for Skiers and Snowboarders

1. Care for others - every skier or snowboard rider must behave so that he does not endanger or cause injury to another.

2. Speed control and riding style - every skier or snowboard rider must be able to see where he is going. He must adapt his speed and style to his ability and the terrain as well as snow and weather conditions and the traffic.

3. Choice of lane - the skier or snowboarder coming from behind must choose a lane such that he does not endanger the skier or snowboarder in front.

4. Overtaking - overtaking may be done from above or below, on the right or the left, but always leaving room to allow the skier or snowboarder being overtaken to carry out any movements required.

5. Entering and exiting - the skier or snowboarder who enters a slope or wishes to continue down the slope after a halt must check up and down the slope that he can do so without endangering either himself or others.

6. Stopping - every skier or snowboarder must avoid stopping on a narrow part of the slope or at a blind spot, unless in an emergency. A skier or snowboarder who falls at such a place must clear the area as quickly as possible.

7. Climbing up and down - a skier or snowboarder who is climbing up or coming down the slope on foot must use the edge of the piste.

8. Taking notice of signs - each skier or snowboarder must take note of the piste markers and any signals.

9. Help in an emergency - in case of an accident everyone must give aid.

10. Proof of identity - every skier or snowboarder, whether as a witness or being involved, must give his particulars in the event of an accident.

SNOWBOARD

156

(Photo: René Marks)

8 PURE INFORMATION

8.1 Snowboarding Glossary

A
Air, Aerials: Jumping.
Anchor lift: T-bar lift.

B
Backside: On the heel side.
Backside turn: A turn created by placing pressure down on the heels.
Bank: An artificial mound built of snow on a downhill slope.
Basket lift: Ski lift with a plate seat fitted to the end of the T-bar.
Big Foot: A special short ski made by the firm Kneissl.
Board-bag: A bag for keeping the snowboards in.
Boardercross: Freeriding competition involving various different obstacles.

C
Caballerial: A 360º aerial backwards jump.
Camp: A snowboarding course of instruction for youths over several days including fringe events.
Canting: When the binding is angled over.
Carve: A swing turn carried out on the board edges.
Cleats: Metal plates let into the snowboarding boots that clip into the step-in bindings.
Coping: The upper lip of a halfpipe.
Corkscrew: A jump executed over the shoulder, similar to a McTwist.
Cruising: Moving along on the piste in a leisurely fashion.

D
Downhill: A fast slope.
Drifting: When the snowboard skids sideways.

E
Effective edge length: The length of the board edge that actually grips into the snow.

F

Fakie: Moving backwards.
Flat: The flat part between the walls in the halfpipe.
Flex: The flexing capability of the snowboard.
Flip: Rotating in a horizontal direction.
Freecarving board: A board for sports events doing fast turns on the piste.
Freeriding: Moving through open ground.
Freeriding board: An all-round very manoeuvrable board for all types of terrain.
Freestyle board: A board constructed especially for doing tricks and the half-pipe.
Frontside turn: A turn created by placing pressure down on the toes.
Funbox: A freestyle oriented construction in open ground made up of 4 jump ramps which converge onto a central platform.
Funpark: A freestyle area dotted about with various different obstacles and jumps.

G

Gamepad: The control panel for a computer game.
Gap: A freestyle oriented construction in open ground made up of 2 banks (back to back) with a gap in between them.
Giant Slalom: A slalom race where a snowboarder goes down a course of wide-set gates against the clock.
Goofy: Position of the binding on the board; the right foot leads.
Grab: Gripping the edge of the board during a jump.

H

Haaken Flip: A 360° backwards flip jump (named after the creator: Terje HAAKONSEN).
Half-pipe: An elliptical tube shape, artificially formed in the snow.
Handplants: Executing a handstand on the top lip of the half-pipe.
Hard boot: Ski boots made of hard plastic for fitting into the binding plates.
Highback: The rear section of the binding that is formed high up to take the boot.
Hiking: Climbing when freeriding.
Homepages: Web pages on the Internet.

SNOW BOARD

I

Indy Air: A jump where the rear hand grips the forward edge of the board.
Inserts: Screw down points let into the board for mounting the bindings.
Invert: A jump where the head is lower than the board.

K

Kicker: A steep jumping ramp.

L

Late: Delay in executing a trick.
Leash: Safety line connecting the board to the snowboarder's ankle.
Liner: An inner lining to the soft or hardboots.
Lip: The upper edge of a snow mound or drift.

M

McTwist: A vertical 540 º jump (1.5 turns) done in the half-pipe.
Mellow Air: A jump with the forward hand holding the edge of the heel end of the board.
Method Air: A jump with the forward hand holding the edge of the heel end of the board; the front leg is pulled up and the rear leg is stretched out.
Mid-position: The normal basic position when moving on the snowboard.

N

Nose: The tip of the board.
Nose-bone: A jump where the front leg is stretched out and the rear leg is pulled up.
Nose-grab: A jump where the hand grips the tip of the board.
Nose-roll: A twist-turn forward around the tip of the board on the move.

O

Off-the-lip: A turn executed off the top edge of a snow mound or drift.
Ollie: A jump without a ramp, whereby one pushes off by applying pressure at the end of the board.
One Foot Air: A jump where only the forward foot stays in the binding.

P

Pad: An anti-slip protrusion fitted to the board between the two bindings to prevent the foot slipping off the board when using the ski lift.

Parallel-(Giant-) Slalom: A slalom race between two snowboarders through narrow gates.

Plate bindings: A base-plate, with metal clips at the ends to take the snowboarding boots (hardboots), fitted to the board.

Platform: An area or place to stand on the upper edge of the half-pipe.

Powder: Deep snow.

Q

Quarterpipe: A jumping ramp in the shape of half of a half-pipe.

R

Race board: A competition board - not for beginners.

Rails: A balustrade set up in the snow to slide along (also called Slides).

Ramp: A mound or hillock to launch one into a jump.

Regular: Binding position with the left foot forward.

S

Sandboarding: Snowboarding on sand hills - steep slopes are necessary.

Shell bindings: A base-plate mounted on the board with clips, which strap down the boots, mounted on the sides.

Short skis: A climbing aid for freeriders (See Steigfelle).

Side: The edge of the board next to the jump off.

Sidecut: The difference between the broadest and the narrowest part of the board.

Slide: Slipping or sliding diagonally to the direction of movement (e.g., on the rails).

Slopestyle: An obstacle course with various different freestyle elements built into it.

Smithbone: A 180° air jump, executed as a fakie (creator; A. SMITH).

Snow drift: Snow, whipped up by the wind into a bank; can be used as a jumping ramp.

Snow irons: Climbing aids for freeriding (mounted on the boots).

Snurfer: Snowboard originally patented by Sherman POPPEN.

Soft boots: Soft boots for snowboards with shell bindings.

Spin: Rotation in a horizontal direction.
Stalefish: A jump where the rear hand grips the heel edge of the board between the legs with the rear leg stretched out.
Steigfelle: Overlays for short skis designed to improve the grip when climbing.
Step-in-system: Bindings with a click-in system similar to ski bindings.
Straps: The clips on the shell bindings.
Stylephase: The moment in a jump where the snowboarder can insert a trick.
Swallowtail: V-shaped tail end of a powder board.
Swatch Access: Electronic ski pass in the form of a watch made by the Swiss Swatch manufacturer.

T
Tail: End of the board.
Tail-bone: A jump where the rear leg is stretched out and the forward one is pulled up.
Tail grab: A jump where the hand grips the end of the snowboard.
Touring snowboards: A snowboard for freeriders that can be taken apart into two pieces and used as two short boards for climbing.
Transition: Crossover from the flat to the vertical part of the pipe.

V
Vert: Vertical section of the wall in the pipe.

W
Wakeboard: Sports equipment, similar to a snowboard, for use on water behind a motorboat and on special cable-ways.
Wheelie: Moving along on only the tip or the end of the snowboard.
Wristguard: Protection for the wrist (as for inline skating).

8.2 Internet Addresses

Snowboarding-Associations
ISF International – www.isf.ch
FIS – www.fissnowboarding.com

Snowboarding Magazine
ONBOARD Snowboard Magazine – www.onboardmag.com
Snowboarding ONLINE – www.solsnowboarding.com

Snowboarding – Camps and Events
SWATCH BoarderX World Tour – www.boarderx.com
Stryn Summer Camps – www.snowboard.no

Snowboarding – Miscellaneous
Nicola Thost Private – www.nicolathost.de
Austrian Tourist Information – www.tiscover.com
Nitro Snowboards – www.nitro.de
Ski Resorts – Ski Guide – www.skiresort.de
Swatch-Watches – www.swatch.com
Raichle Boots – www.raichle.com
F2 Snowboards – www.f2.com
Adidas Eye Protection – www.adidas-ep.com
K2 Snowboards – www.k2snowboards.com

Snowboarding Games
XGames Proboarder – www.proboarder.com
Big Air – www.playstation-europe.com
Cool Boarders 1,2,3 – www.playstation-europe.com
Twisted Edge Extreme Snowboarding – www.nintendosports.com

Wakeboarding
WAKEBOARDING Online-USA – www.wakeworld.com

Sandboarding
Sandboard Magazine – www.sandboard.com

Acknowledgements

The authors of this book wish to thank the following companies for their excellent co-operation:

NITRO Snowboards
Nitro Snowboards Handels GmbH
F2 Snowboards
F2 International Vertriebs GmbH
RAICHLE Snowboardboots
Raichle Boots AG
ADIDAS Eye Protection
Silhouette Vertriebs GmbH
PRIMA PRINT
Druck & Verlag GmbH
SWATCH Uhren
The Swatch Group Deutschland GmbH
ODLO Functional Fashion
Odlo International AG
K2 Snowboards
K2 Sportartikel GmbH
FANATIC Sportswear
Ultra Trend Vertriebs GmbH
CICLOcontrol Uhren
Ciclosport K.W. Hochschorner GmbH

Thanks also to, in particular, Andrea Münster, Sven Seliger, Senta Reith, Markus Luckey, Claudia Hellstern, Thomas Latein, Monika Maurer, Frau Stehrenberger, Oliver Heimbach, and the staff of Prima Print.

It has been fun working together with you on this book. Thanks go also to Achim Schmidt, Nicole Zahn-Bechen, Chantal Liegel, David Steinbach, Frank Runge and Robin Koch.

Photo & Illustration Credits

Cover Photo: René Marks
Cover Design: Birgit Engelen
Photos & Illustrations: see credits underneath each photo

Fit for the Winter …

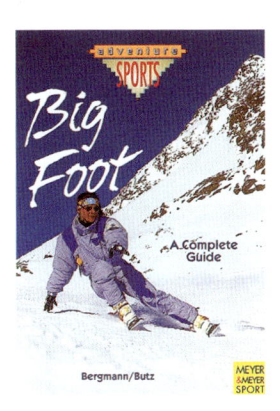

wintersport

Adventure Sports
Stefan Bergmann/Christian Butz
Big Foot
A Complete Guide

BIG FOOT is the name for specially designed short skis which have become the latest craze in winter fun.
This exciting new technology is easily learned and enjoyed by beginners yet offers the more experienced a wide scope for performing stunts and tricks. This complete guide to BIG FOOT tells you, in an appealing and often humorous style, everything you need to know to get started and quickly develop your BIG FOOT skills.

144 pages
Full-colour print
65 colour photos
Paperback, 14.8 x 21 cm
ISBN 3-89124-497-5
£ 14.95 UK/
$ 19.95 US/$ 29.95 CDN

MEYER & MEYER SPORT

MEYER & MEYER Verlag · Von-Coels-Straße 390 · D-52080 Aachen, Germany · Fax +49 (0)2 41-9 58 10-10

Fit for the Winter...

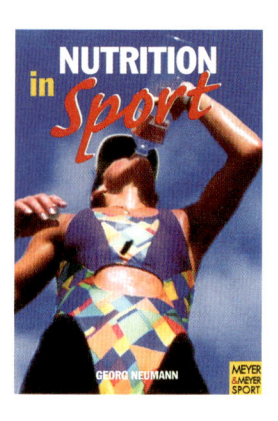

Wintersport

Georg Neumann
Nutrition in Sport

The book makes recommendations for physiologically useful dietary planning before, during and after training in various sports.
It also examines risk-prone groups in sports nutrition.
The emphasis is on presenting the latest research on the effects of carbohydrates and proteins and other active substances, such as vitamins and minerals, on performance training. Particular attention is paid to the intake of food and fluids under special conditions such as training in heat, in the cold and at high altitudes.

208 pages
Two-colour print
Some full-colour photos
Paperback, 14.8 x 21 cm
ISBN 1-84126-003-7
£ 12.95 UK/
$ 17.95 US/$ 25.95 CDN

MEYER & MEYER SPORT

MEYER & MEYER Verlag | Von-Coels-Straße 390 | D-52080 Aachen, Germany | Fax +49 (0)2 41-9 58 10-10

Fit for the Winter...

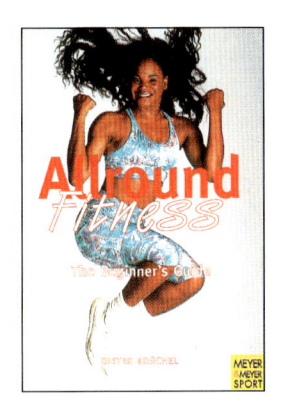

Dieter Koschel
Allround Fitness
The Beginner's Guide

„Allround Fitness" by Dieter Koschel explains his popular and proven approach to fitness, incorporating both basic training principles and the all important element of fun. Designed as a guide for fitness instructors, teachers and personal training, the book describes a well thought out, basic programme consisting of gymnastic exercises, cardio vascular training and relaxation techniques.

120 pages
37 photos
17 figures and 10 tables
Paperback, 14.8 x 21 cm
ISBN 1-84126-011-8
£ 9.95 UK/
$ 14.95 US/$ 20.95 CDN

MEYER & MEYER SPORT

MEYER & MEYER SPORT

Please order our catalogue!
Please order our catalogue!

„Snowboarding"
is just one example of our varied sports programme.

Meyer & Meyer
publishes many other English titles under the following categories:

▼

Aerobic ■ Bodywork ■ Endurance
Fitness & Recreation ■ Fun
Games & Sports ■ Golf ■ Gymnastics
Health ■ Martial Arts ■ Rowing
Running ■ Soccer ■ Surfing ■ Tennis
Triathlon & Duathlon
Volleyball ■ Winter Sports

Meyer & Meyer also publishes various international journals and a series of scientific sports titles.

If you are interested in **Meyer & Meyer Sport** and our large programme, please visit us **online** or call our **Hotline** ▼

online:
▶ www.meyer-meyer-sports.com

▶ Hotline:
+49 (0)1 80 / 5 10 11 15

We are looking forward to your call!

MEYER & MEYER Verlag | Von-Coels-Straße 390 | D-52080 Aachen, Germany | Fax +49 (0)2 41 - 9 58 10-10